Marilyn

NEIL
SINYARD

LONGMEADOW
PRESS

PAGE 1: The ultimate example of movie glamour: Marilyn Monroe.

PAGE 2: Marilyn on the beach, as captured by one of her closest photographer friends, Sam Shaw.

RIGHT: A pensive Marilyn on the set of *Let's Make Love* in 1960.

FAR RIGHT: Marilyn in pin-up pose during the making of *How To Marry a Millionaire* in 1953.

This 1992 edition published by
Longmeadow Press
201 High Ridge Road
Stamford CT 06904

Produced by
Brompton Books Corporation
15 Sherwood Place
Greenwich CT 06830

ISBN 0-681-41593-2

Printed in Hong Kong

0 9 8 7 6 5 4 3

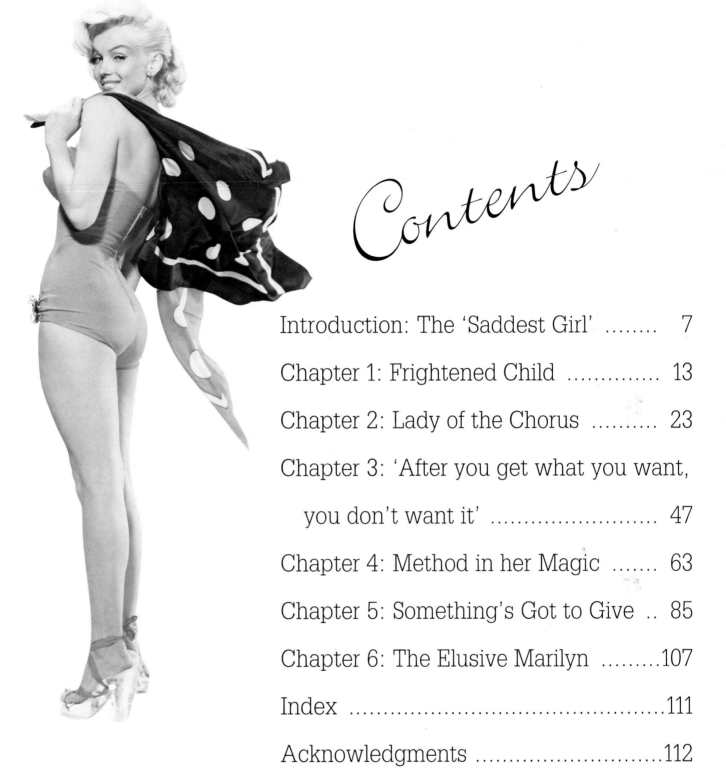

Contents

Introduction

THE 'SADDEST GIRL'

'My God, I think there have been more books on Marilyn Monroe than on World War Two – and there's a great similarity.' BILLY WILDER

She consorted with and was wooed by presidents, from America to Indonesia. As a co-star, she enraged then upstaged Sir Laurence Olivier. She married not one but two American legends in vastly different areas of endeavor; one of the country's greatest baseball heroes, Joe DiMaggio, and one of its foremost dramatists, Arthur Miller.

She was the subject of a modern art classic of Andy Warhol, of a song by Elton John ('Candle in the Wind') and two books by Norman Mailer. She captured the heart of a venerable poet like Robert Frost; the philosopher Jean-Paul Sartre thought her the finest actress alive; and she had a signed photograph of Albert Einstein (though closer inspection has revealed the handwriting to be Eli Wallach's).

Yet she came from a family background with enough skeletons to rattle two cupboards and with a mad and melodramatic intensity that might have fazed Tennessee Williams. Her rise to celebrity from such unpromising origins might therefore seem like

FAR LEFT: That smile, that dress: Marilyn in the kind of shot that was to entrance audiences the world over.

LEFT: A Cecil Beaton photograph that caught a more melancholy Marilyn. He was to describe her as being as 'spectacular as the silvery shower of a Vesuvius fountain.'

a contemporary fairy-tale, an affirmation of the kind of upward mobility only possible in our century. At a famous Hollywood banquet she attended for Soviet Premier Kruschev, Spyros Skouras was boasting patriotically of his rise from carpet salesman to president of Twentieth Century Fox. 'Well,' Kruschev replied, 'I was the son of a coal miner and look at *me*.' She thought that a marvellous reply and in her final interview she was to insist that it was the people who had made her a star – no studio, no one person, but the common people.

In one sense she was a gorgeous embodiment of the American Dream, but arguably at the cost of having to endure a nightmare of the soul. Her biography was indeed a kind of fairy-story but of an unusually poignant kind. For one thing, it had an unhappy ending. She was a Cinderella who not only finally went to the Ball but triumphed as never before. But this Cinderella existed in a neurotic age. No Prince Charming successfully materialized and, when midnight struck one fateful night, this reigning princess of the dream factory found herself utterly alone.

Her life is one of the most sensational of the century. One exasperated researcher for *Life* magazine called her biography a 'pathological detective story.' He was writing this before the turbulent and traumatic final years, in which the story stretched beyond the treacherous waters of showbiz and into the minefields of conspiratorial power-politics. Who could have guessed that the subject of the most celebrated pin-up story of the 1950s would also be the subject of one of the 1960s' most sinister cover-ups?

Arthur Miller felt her 'catastrophe' was rooted in 'her having been condemned from birth – cursed might be a better word.' Yet if this were so, her enigmatic death is far less significant than her extraordinary and exhilarating life. If she were the plaything of fate from the day she was born (and it is Miller who gives her that anguished line in *The Misfits* [1961], 'We're dying, aren't we . . . every minute'), by what miracle did she scale the heights she did?

In Miller's words, she was 'like champagne on the screen.' For men, because of her voluptuous beauty, she was the ultimate screen goddess. For women, because of the comedy and vulnerability she projected behind this fabulous façade, she seemed a precious vessel of fragile femininity in a ruthless world. Perhaps for psychiatry, she was an unfathomable case-history. For posterity, she remains simply the ultimate movie star.

There could never be another Marilyn Monroe. This is her story.

LEFT and BELOW: Marilyn during her modelling years. She was the darling of the photographers, appearing on the cover of five different magazines in one month in 1946.

BELOW: Marilyn at the press conference of *Some Like It Hot* in 1959.

RIGHT: Natural Beauty: Marilyn in 1954.

Chapter One

FRIGHTENED CHILD

The Early Years of Norma Jeane (1926-1946)

'Poor Marilyn was a scared girl, scared of everything. God knows why she was so frightened.' FRITZ LANG

She was born Norma Jeane Mortensen in Los Angeles General Hospital on 1 June 1926, under the sign of Gemini. Marilyn had a lifelong interest in astrology and she always saw this birthdate as significant. For example, the letter 'G' seemed to her to play a disproportionately important role in her life: a mother called Gladys, a guardian called Grace, a family called the Giffens who wanted to adopt her, a suspected father called Gifford, a business partner called Greene, and, of course, an ultimate screen hero of hers called Gable.

To Marilyn Gemini also meant, as she told an interviewer, 'Jekyll and Hyde. Two in one.' She could certainly be that. Director George Cukor talked of her being quite maddening one minute and quite adorable the next. Arthur Miller remembers a slashing temper that could moderate with disconcerting rapidity to sweetness directed at the same person, as if she had entirely forgotten the reason for her fury. Laurence Olivier bluntly called her 'schizoid: the two people that she was could hardly be more different.'

The secret of Marilyn's nature was not only in her stars, of course, but in the circumstances of a broken home. Her mother was Gladys Pearl Baker Mortensen. Born in 1902, by the time of Norma Jeane's birth, she had been married twice and had two children by her previous marriage, now being raised by relatives of her first husband. The father of the little girl was almost certainly not Gladys's husband, Martin E Mortensen, who seems to have left her shortly after they married in 1924. It is more generally believed that the girl's father was a film laboratory salesman, C Stanley Gif-

ford, who had been Gladys's lover but who did not want to marry her. He would never acknowledge the child as his, and an attempt by her in 1952 (by this time famous as Marilyn Monroe) to effect a reconciliation ended in humiliation and bitter rejection. Small wonder that friends, lovers, even film audiences, could also sense deep within the beautiful woman that was Marilyn Monroe the child that was Norma Jeane.

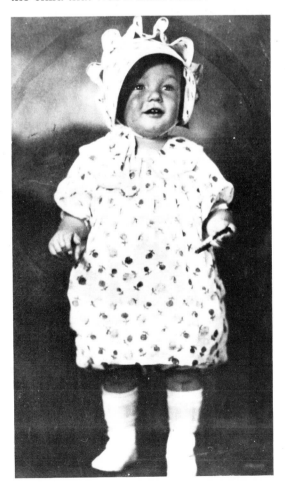

LEFT: What the well-dressed toddler should wear: Marilyn during the period when she was being fostered by the Bolenders.

FAR LEFT: A publicity picture of Marilyn as babysitter taken in 1949, a poignant photograph in the light of her later frustrated desire for a baby of her own.

One of the dominant memories of Marilyn's childhood was that as a girl she would stare at a picture of Gifford that hung on the living-room wall, struck by his striking resemblance to Clark Gable, ironically to be her final co-star. She remembered fantasizing that Gable might be her actual father; and one might imagine the impact on her if she saw a young star of about her own age, Judy Garland in *Broadway Melody of 1938* (1937) when she sang 'Dear Mr Gable' to a photograph of the star.

Here real-life becomes curiously entangled with Marilyn's screen image. In her life, she was always drawn to older men and curiously, in her films, nearly all her screen lovers are old enough to be her father. Not that she had exclusive control over casting; yet when she did have the opportunity to play opposite one of Hollywood's younger leading men – when, for example, Rock Hudson was being considered for the role of the cowboy in *Bus Stop* (1956) – she hesitated long enough for him to drop out of the picture. The child-woman *persona* she cultivated in her movies seems intimately linked to the father complex she trailed throughout her life. 'Every Baby Needs a Da Da Daddy' she sings in *Ladies of the Chorus* (1948). 'My Heart Belongs to Daddy' she croons in *Let's Make Love* (1960). Certainly her scenes with Gable in *The Misfits* (1961) seem the most heartfelt romantic scenes she played in the movies. Coincidentally, as a young starlet in *All About Eve* (1950) Marilyn drools over a sable coat and remarks: 'Now there's something a girl could make sacrifices for.' 'Did you say sable, or Gable?' asks a producer, to which Marilyn rejoins: 'Either one.'

Marilyn's father-fixation was one effect of her broken home, but it was not the only one, nor was it the most serious. The most unsettling ingredient in her environment was the family's history of mental instability. Insanity and suicide run through Marilyn's ancestry, together with religious fanaticism. For George Cukor this was the final explanation for Marilyn's character and behavior: 'Truth to tell, I think she was quite mad.'

Her great-grandfather had hanged himself at the age of eighty-two. Her grandmother, Della Monroe (whose name Marilyn was, perhaps ominously, to adopt) had been a fanatical follower of the controversial evangelist Aimee Semple McPherson: indeed, as a young girl Marilyn was actually baptized in McPherson's temple. Distressed by the scandal that erupted when Miss McPherson disappeared (was it a kidnapping, as she claimed, or a sordid love tryst?), Della gradually became mentally unhinged and was committed to an institution on 4 August 1927, thirty-five years to the day prior to Marilyn's death. Within three weeks of being committed, Della had died of heart failure. Much later in Marilyn's life, even her guardian Grace Goddard was to commit suicide, but for the child, undoubtedly, the most distressing manifestation of the family's mental history was the condition of her mother. Gladys Mortensen's recurrent nervous breakdowns made it impossible for her to look after her daughter for any consistent stretch of time. This led to the child being cared for by friends, relatives, ten different foster homes, and, for nearly two years, in the Los Angeles Orphans' Home. For practically the whole of her early life, the young girl had to be nervously dependent on what Blanche DuBois, in her last line of Tennessee Williams's *A Streetcar Named Desire*, unforgettably calls 'the kindness of strangers.'

During the early stages of Marilyn's stardom, the story arose that she was an orphan. Rather like the embarrassingly eccentric mother of the child-star in Gavin Lambert's Hollywood novel, *Inside Daisy Clover* (subsequently made into a film in 1965), the mother was safely hidden away in an obscure institution, and studio publicity had it that her father had been killed in a car crash shortly after she was born. For gossip columnists like Hedda Hopper and Louella Parsons, her stardom was therefore a marvellous triumph of fate and a wonderful advertisement for Hollywood warm-heartedness since she had been brought up in filmland's very own orphanage. Later, when the existence of Marilyn's mother was discovered, the story had to be revised by the studio publicists. By that time, though, the myth was so powerful that Marilyn's orphan status continued to be insisted on by a section of the press despite blatant evidence to the contrary. The young girl's perception of that status was a good deal less romantic. Marilyn would remember for years afterwards being dragged into the Home, screaming 'I'm not an orphan! I'm not an orphan!'

It is probably difficult to exaggerate the feelings of rejection experienced by a child in that situation, knowing her parents are alive but who cannot, or will not, take care of her. There were undoubtedly terrifying moments in her early life when she must have felt completely abandoned. These moments became unhealed scars, particularly when the pattern began to repeat itself in her adulthood. It culminated in her lonely death on a Saturday night. 'Her first night in the orphanage,' said Arthur Miller, 'must have withered up the blessing of life and it

RIGHT: Marilyn as a little girl. Her young playmate is a boy, Lester, who was to be adopted by the Bolenders.

she projects an aura of waif more than wife and seems someone to be protected as well as desired.

She had, then, inherited a legacy of family madness that would not have seemed out of place in a drama by Ibsen or O'Neill. How does someone cope with a background like that? Probably either through a quest for love or through a retreat into fantasy. If the former failed, then the latter was a strong option. It would, of course, be a dangerous option in Marilyn's case, given her family's mental history.

Fantasy seems to have expressed itself in two particular ways in her childhood. The first was something that was familiar to many people during the years of the Depression for a wide variety of reasons: a fascination with the glamour of the movies as a temporary escape from grim reality. Woody Allen has dramatized this feeling with great comedy and poignancy in *The Purple Rose of Cairo* (1985). The young Norma Jeane was a particularly big fan of Gable and Jean Harlow and, even as a teenager, she would act out roles in her bedroom and discover a talent for being able to cry on cue. For a child in Los Angeles, the Hollywood fantasy must have seemed a little less remote, a little more within reaching distance, than for other children.

Indeed, the movies were impinging on Marilyn's life from a very early age. Before her recurrent bouts of mental illness, her mother had been a negative cutter at Columbia and RKO. At one stage, too, she had rented their house to a British couple, one of whom was employed as a stand-in for the eminent stage and screen actor, George Arliss. The couple looked after Marilyn for a while after her mother's breakdown in 1934 but, when Arliss decided to return to England, the couple returned also, precipitating a set of circumstances which would eventually lead the young Norma Jeane to be placed in the LA Orphanage from 1935 to 1937. Yet even there the child could look out of her room window and see the soundstages and famous watch-tower of the RKO Studios, no doubt hardly daring to think of a time in the future when she might be working there. On this first level of fantasy, the young girl's dream of glamour and escape was to come true. It happened seventeen years later. On RKO's *Clash by Night* (1952) reporters would be brusquely brushing past a great star like Barbara Stanwyck to get a word with 'the new girl with the big tits.'

The second level of fantasy about Marilyn's life is much more ambiguous. It has to do with events that generally embroider the impression of Marilyn's tough early life but which may or may not have actually hap-

died in her there.' It explained, Miller thought, Marilyn's special warmth towards his father, who was an orphan. It also explained her ability to sense in a crowd those people who had lost parents in childhood, an instinct that, according to him, was uncanny and unerring.

Inevitably this experience would build up a tormenting duality in Marilyn: an enormous desire for love contending with an overwhelming wariness of it, for fear it would again lead to the horror of abandonment. Everyone who knew her sensed her love for and ease with old people and children, who shared her vulnerability and could do her no harm. With nearly everyone else, she was wary and withdrawn, fearing to trust and constantly putting love through the kind of tests that can only poison and destroy it. Again it is a mysterious quality picked up in her film performances, where

ABOVE: Marilyn and her first husband, Jim Dougherty, during their period in Catalina in 1944.

There are things I remember that may never have happened but, as I recall them, so they take place.' Marilyn's memory seems to have worked a little like that. Commissioned to write her life story in 1954, the redoubtable cynic and screenwriter, Ben Hecht, found much of it hard to believe. He did not think Marilyn was trying to deceive him, she was simply an incorrigible fantasizer. On a similar assignment in 1956, the veteran Hollywood correspondent for *Time* magazine, Ezra Goodman, was equally baffled, finding a morass of contradictory material that even then seemed closer to Raymond Chandler than convincing fact. In the event, *Time* magazine ran a story that Goodman felt was a travesty of his research but perpetuated yet another myth: little Orphan Annie makes good in Hollywood.

There are several shocking stories about her childhood that have acquired a certain veracity and authenticity (they appear in most film encyclopedias outlining Marilyn's biography, for example) but which are hard to verify. Did her grandmother really attempt to suffocate her when the child was only 13 months old? Marilyn repeatedly asserted it and Arthur Miller for one firmly believed it, but skeptics insist that adults just do not have such clear memories of events that early in childhood. Was Marilyn raped as a child? To different reporters, she said she was raped at the age of six, or nine, or eleven, or fourteen, but most research has turned up only two instances of unpleasant physical molestation by adults, which nevertheless stopped well short of rape. Did Marilyn have a baby when she was a teenager, and feel guilty ever after about giving it away? She told this story to her former maid, Lena Pepitone, who published it to general incredulity in her memories of Marilyn. Yet she also told it to Amy, the wife of her business partner Milton Greene. The problem was that the baby was born in different years in the two versions, and neither of the women could decide whether the story was true or false, both feeling that it might be a punishment-fantasy of Marilyn's prompted by her inability in adulthood to conceive.

It is extraordinary that a life lived so much in the public gaze should nevertheless be so mysterious, both before and after her death. The mysteries throw disturbing shadows over Marilyn's sanity if she truly believed those things she had only imagined; and yet if they were true and she was not believed, her sense of rejection and isolation must have been quite unbearable.

In a series of articles in 1956 entitled 'The Unknown Monroe' (erroneously subtitled 'The little orphan who became Big Busi-

pened. Much of this was the work of paid publicists or gossip columnists, who wished to add a touch of lurid drama to an already sensational story. Yet Marilyn herself seems partially to have collaborated in the myths about her childhood, to the point where it might have become as difficult for her as anyone else to distinguish imagination from fact.

In Harold Pinter's wonderful play about time, memory and illusion, *Old Times*, the character Anna says at one stage: 'There are some things one remembers even though they may never have happened.

LEFT: On the Twentieth Century Fox lot in 1947, shortly after signing her first contract.

ness'), the British newspaper *Daily Herald* described her early life as resembling 'the plot of a social novel by Charles Dickens' and talked of her being hit with a razor strap if she answered back. The portrait of the orphanage as something out of *Nicholas Nickleby*, and of her early guardians, the Bolenders, as sadistic more than strict, probably made good copy, but it is an exaggeration of the truth. Nevertheless, one must not undervalue the unsettling impact on the young girl of so many different surrogate parents. In adult life, it was to lead to her 'adopting,' as it were, a succession of different families, who would look after her for a few months, or longer, before she drifted on: the Carrolls in the 1940s; the Greenes and the Strasbergs in the 1950s; and, in the final years of her life, the family of her psychiatrist, Dr Ralph Greenson. Her official guardian during her childhood was a friend of her mother, Grace McKee, but it was not until after Grace had been married to 'Doc' Goddard, that she was finally able to take the child into her home in 1938.

One acknowledged incident that has given rise to much comment is the time when a drunken 'Doc' Goddard burst into the young girl's room and kissed her passionately, sliding his tongue into her mouth. Was this one of Marilyn's fantasy rapes? Was it an incident that prompted Grace to arrange a quick marriage for her to the first available eligible man, who happened to be one of the sons of their neighbors, the 17-year-old James Dougherty? According to *Time* magazine in 1952, Marilyn was married at the age of 16 to Dougherty, on 19 June 1942, 'to avoid being sent to an orphanage.' This seems an overstatement of the case. There was an initial mutual attraction and a fair amount of happiness in the early stages of marriage. Dougherty worked at an aircraft plant and, according to a co-worker, was delighted with his young wife and would show off a photograph of her in which she was wearing nothing but an apron and a smile. This co-worker, incidentally, was Robert Mitchum who, a decade later, was to be reunited with Marilyn in *River of No Return* (1954). 'Marilyn and I are a lot alike,' he was to say. 'There's not one single day when we can do one single thing gracefully. We're always in the soup.'

What seems to have divided the couple eventually was their immaturity – they were both too young for the responsibility and commitment of marriage, and the unstable situation provoked by the War. Dougherty's application to enlist in the Navy brought back all of the young girl's old fears of abandonment. When he was eventually shipped out, the marriage began to head toward the rocks.

They had moved to Catalina in 1943, and she had gone to work at an aircraft factory,

LEFT: Marilyn in playful
mood by the sea.

BELOW: Gone fishing:
Marilyn on a modelling
assignment in 1946.

packing parachutes. It was there she was discovered by an Army photographer, David Conover, who worked for the First Motion Picture Unit in Hal Roach Studios. Conover had been sent to the factory to do some 'morale-boosting' shots of women at work in wartime for *Yank* magazine. The photographs came to the attention of the head of the Blue Book Modelling Studio and Agency, and Norma Jeane was offered a modelling job. She was an immediate success. Her assignments led to numerous appearances on magazine covers and calendars – in 1946, she appeared on the cover of five magazines in one month. The assignments also led to a determination to secure a divorce from Dougherty.

There are some observers who insist to this day that Marilyn was a better model than actress, and that more of the essence and magic of Monroe was revealed in still photographs than ever came through on celluloid. 'In her films she is like an unripe orange,' claims the critic David Thomson, 'heavy with unfulfilled inwardness, a sunless yellow, hard and green at the poles. But in her still photographs, she is the fruit cut open, the juice about to jump in your eyes.' 'She would always do exactly what was asked of her by any stills photographer,' said Laurence Olivier, 'I marvelled at first at this show of discipline and thought it augured well; my reaction a few weeks later would have been '' Well, of course – a model.''' Both judgments seem excessively surly and uncharitable, considerably underestimating what even some of Marilyn's most exasperated collaborators conceded were her considerable comic and dramatic gifts. It is inconceivable that she could have had a comparable impact on the basis of a modelling career.

And yet at this stage there is one other mystery about the early life of Marilyn Monroe that is still elusive and has never been satisfactorily explained. Given that it was clear that she now could have made a lucrative career for herself as a model, when and where and why did she conceive the idea of going into movies? For this is what she did. When she divorced Dougherty in 1946 and when her mother, who had been staying with her for the first seven months of that year, finally returned to the sanatorium and to a life of permanent institutionalization, she began to storm Hollywood. The stage was set for a new appearance, a new identity and a new life, all perhaps in the hope that the shadows of her past could at last be shaken off. This was to prove more difficult than she thought for stardom brought in its wake a host of new problems which would bring back all her childhood fears.

ABOVE: A picture of Marilyn taken during the filming of *Hometown Story* in 1951, a non-theatrical release that advertised the virtues of American industry.

LEFT: Marilyn in 1952.

FAR LEFT: Marilyn displays the elegance of a Lana Turner.

Chapter Two

LADY OF THE CHORUS
The Emergence of Marilyn Monroe (1946-1952)

'Blonde, pneumatic, full of peasant health. Just the type for me!' GEORGE SANDERS

Marilyn's erratic and erotic path to stardom took approximately six years to traverse. It was an eventful journey. It included a possible abortion, an attempted suicide, a near-rape, a new name, extensive cosmetic surgery, enthusiastic re-education, a low-point of being dropped by two studios before being reclaimed and a high-point of a nude calendar pose that provoked some of the most salacious publicity in Hollywood's entire history.

There were three main factors in Marilyn's rise to public prominence during this period. The first was the publicity and attention generated by her modelling and public appearances. The second was the support of significant patrons who, sometimes out of artistic unselfishness but often out of love and desire, helped her to secure roles and improve her performances. The third was her appearance during this time in no fewer than 14 movies. Of these three factors, undoubtedly the least significant were the movies in which she appeared. This is not to say that they were all bad. Some were good, and three – John Huston's *The Asphalt Jungle* (1950), Joseph L Mankiewicz's *All About Eve* (1950) and Howard Hawks' *Monkey Business* (1952) – are enduring classics. Their quality, however, had comparatively little to do with the presence of Marilyn Monroe in them.

The talent scout at Twentieth Century Fox, Ben Lyon (a former screen actor and later a popular radio performer), never tired of recounting his memory of the day of 16 July 1946 when his secretary informed him that a young girl called Norma Jeane wished to see him and this apparition floated into his office. 'She was absolutely gorgeous,' said Lyon, 'dressed in a beautifully cut, inexpensive cotton print with her golden hair down to her shoulders. I must admit I had never seen anyone so attractive. I asked what she wanted and she replied she wanted to get into pictures and I remember exactly my answer, it was "Honey, you're in pictures".' Lyon arranged for a screen test to be directed by the experienced director Walter Lang (who would later direct Marilyn in *There's No Business Like Show Business* [1954]) and photographed by the Oscar-winning cameraman, Leon Shamroy. Darryl Zanuck, the head of the studio, liked the test and agreed the standard studio optional seven-year contract, renewable every six months. (This meant that the studio could drop any actor or actress within any six month period of the seven years, but the actor or actress had no reciprocal rights of that kind.) According to Lyon, Marilyn wept with gratitude when she heard the terms of the contract: $175 per week for the first six months, rising to $1500 a week by the seventh year. Later she would weep with frustration at a contract whose terms had been far outstripped by the scale of her stardom.

As with many young aspiring starlets, the first thing the studio suggested was a change of name. It was Ben Lyon who suggested 'Marilyn,' after a favorite Broadway musical star of his, Marilyn Miller. She suggested 'Monroe' after the name of her grandparents. So Marilyn Monroe was born and Norma Jeane was, it was hoped, dead. The studio assisted the burial by providing a biography for its new star that might have emanated from its Story Department as it did not bear much relation to the truth.

FAR LEFT: Marilyn in 1947: she was soon to be known as the queen of bathing beauty art.

ABOVE: Marilyn (at the front of the rowing boat) in *Scudda Hoo! Scudda Hay!* (1948), officially her screen debut, though her only line was cut and her solitary appearance is in long shot.

The studio also tested her in two small roles. In *Scudda Hoo! Scudda Hay!* (1948), Marilyn allegedly appeared in a single long shot and had one word of dialogue 'Hello!' – 'allegedly' because even this fleeting appearance was cut out of the picture. In *Dangerous Years* (1948), a cautionary tale about juvenile delinquency, she had a little more screen time for she played a waitress in a soda shop. Her most significant line was: 'And now you're blowing it on two cokes!' At this point, when the second six months of her contract were up, the studio saw fit not to renew it, and Marilyn went back to modelling.

If she was not exactly an overnight success, Marilyn's life during 1947, by her own account, was lacking in everything but incident. According to her, she was surprised one night in her home by an intruder and ran screaming for her life but when she reported the matter to the police, one of the policemen assigned to the case was recognized by her as the intruder himself. According to Orson Welles, the two had a short-lived affair, ending abruptly at a Hollywood party when their love-making in an upstairs bedroom was interrupted by an irate husband who had mistaken Marilyn for his wife.

According to a mutual friend, Marilyn also had a brief affair at this time with Charlie Chaplin Jr (with whom she was to remain good friends until the end of her life), became pregnant by him and had an abortion in the winter of 1947.

Although her career was proceeding less melodramatically than her private life, there were two developments at this time of some significance. With her fees being paid for by the studio, Marilyn attended classes at Morris Carnofsky's Actors' Lab, a drama school off Sunset Boulevard. Carnofsky was a former member of the renowned Group Theater in New York who had established himself as a reputable character actor in movies. Marilyn's brief association with The Actors' Lab seems to hint at a desire to better herself as an actress and was a harbinger of more significant associations with serious dramatic schools, notably the classes with Michael Chekhov and then at Lee Strasberg's Actors' Studio. Also it was the first of Marilyn's associations with an organization that was said to be politically radical. In the nervous anti-Communist atmosphere of the late 1940s, former membership of the Group Theater was practically synonymous with subversion, and

Carnofsky was later to be blacklisted after being 'named' as a Communist Party member to the House of UnAmerican Activities Committee (HUAC). Marilyn's later, more intimate association with the liberal Arthur Miller was to attract HUAC attention – and, to the end of her life, FBI and CIA surveillance. Marilyn never made any secret of her left-wing sympathies, and part of her later bond with the Kennedys was undoubtedly borne out of her dislike for Richard Nixon, whom she associated with the persecution of her husband, Arthur Miller, during the 1950s.

The second significant development was the relationship she developed with the renowned Hollywood mogul, Joseph M Schenck, who, at the time he spotted Marilyn in 1947, was 70 years old and an executive producer at Twentieth Century Fox. During his career, Schenck had at various times guided the career of Buster Keaton, been president of United Artists, and founded Twentieth Century Studios with Darryl Zanuck before the merger with Fox, at which point he had become chairman of the new company. He had also been jailed for an income tax and Union pay-off scandal in 1941, and had only recently been pardoned and had his citizenship restored by President Truman. Marilyn was attracted by this wealth of experience, reflected in his rugged features and a face that, she said, 'was as much the face of a town as of a man. The whole history of Hollywood was in it.'

The precise nature of the relationship remains obscure. Marilyn denied it was sexual, claiming instead that he offered her protection and a temporary home at a difficult period in her life. Certainly if she had been sleeping with him in return for professional favors, she received little benefit, and none at all at the studio in which Schenck had some influence. It seems more one of the number of close relations Marilyn had with older people during her life, and she was genuinely distraught at Schenck's death in 1961.

When asked by Ben Hecht about the 'casting couch' route to stardom, Marilyn replied: 'Hollywood's a place where they'll pay you a thousand dollars for a kiss and fifty cents for your soul.' She added that part of her misfortune was that she had too often declined the former and accepted the latter. 'You can't sleep your way into being a star,' Marilyn told a British writer, 'but it helps. A lot of actresses get their first chance that way. Most of the men are such horrors they deserve all they can get out of them!' Besides, she thought, it was no big deal: nobody ever got cancer from sex. Yet it is clear that Marilyn's cultivation of the company of older men was not simply career opportunism. For psychological reasons already indicated, she was drawn instinctively to father figures. And as her remark about Schenck's 'experienced' face indicates, she was also attracted to men who served her not only as fathers but as teachers. She had embarked on a programme of educational self-improvement at this time, reading up on subjects like anatomy and paintings. The writer-director of *All About Eve* (1950), Joseph L Mankiewicz has said that he first noticed Marilyn when he discovered her on the set carrying a copy of Rainer Maria Rilke's *Letters to a Young Poet*. 'I'd have been less taken aback,' said Mankiewicz, 'to come upon Herr Rilke studying a Marilyn Monroe nude calendar.'

In other words, there had to be a genuine attraction on Marilyn's side: she did discriminate between moguls and ogres. There is a story that she was fired from Columbia in 1948 because Harry Cohn, the studio head, had invited her for a weekend on his yacht, an invitation she refused on learning that it did not also include Mrs Cohn. Cohn himself always claimed that she was fired because 'she couldn't act.' After Marilyn's rise to fame, Cohn was unmercifully ribbed by the more courageous of his employees and associates, to the point where he could stand it no longer. 'Get me another blonde who can be a star,' said Cohn – at which point, enter Kim Novak.

Marilyn had landed a contract with Columbia because Schenck had recommended her to Cohn who agreed to give her a chance. She was given a leading role in a B-picture called *Ladies of the Chorus* (1948) and was to play the part of a dancer who is appearing in the same chorus as her mother (Adele Jergens). Marilyn had two songs in the film, 'Anybody Can Tell I Love You' and (the significantly entitled) 'Every Baby Needs a Da Da Daddy,' and Cohn insisted that she do an audition of them in his office with Columbia's musical arranger, Fred Karger. The audition was going badly until, in her nervousness, Marilyn dropped her copy of the *Christian Science Monitor* from a folder of music she was carrying. At this time Marilyn was a keen student of Christian Science, having been influenced by the advocacy of her guardian's aunt, Ana Lower, to whom Marilyn was devoted. Coincidentally, Cohn's wife had taken up Christian Science and he himself had dabbled in it. From that moment on, his tone became noticeably more conciliatory and helpful, and Marilyn's part in the film was assured.

Ladies of the Chorus was to be the only film she made at Columbia but she met two

RIGHT: Ready for the
beach.

LEFT: Casual elegance:
Marilyn in 1950.

people there who made a big impact on her life. The first was Fred Karger, who was on the music staff. Karger is probably best known today for writing the hit song inspired by the film *From Here to Eternity*, for Frank Sinatra, and for marrying, divorcing and then briefly re-marrying Jane Wyman after her divorce from Ronald Reagan. However, all this took place after his traumatic affair with Monroe. His tutelage of her was notably sympathetic and, ever vulnerable to masculine kindness, Marilyn fell deeply in love with him. However, Karger had no desire to marry an insecure, unknown actress; like almost everyone else, he had barely an inkling of Marilyn's potential for stardom. (Even as experienced an eye as the veteran Frank Capra was dismissive at this time when she was brought to his attention: 'Breasts she had. And a wiggly figure. But to me sex is class, something more than a wiggly behind . . . But how could I have passed up Marilyn Monroe?') The relationship drifted painfully, Marilyn aware of its failure but still too much in love to break it off conclusively: 'it was like rushing to the edge of a roof to jump off.' It was an affair that bruised her already fragile belief in male

RIGHT: Marilyn as photographed by the eminent Hungarian-born photographer, Andre de Dienes, whom Marilyn accompanied on a photographic safari over the Christmas of 1945, much to her husband's – at that time James Dougherty – annoyance.

trust-worthiness and fidelity. By one of those strange coincidences with which Marilyn's life and death are littered, Karger was to die in 1979 on the seventeenth anniversary of Marilyn's own death.

The second key figure to make a large impact on Marilyn's life was Columbia's chief drama coach, Natasha Lytess, to whom Marilyn was sent to prepare for her role in *Ladies of the Chorus*. An artistic refugee from Nazi Germany, where she had worked with the Max Reinhardt theater company, Natasha was much older than Marilyn and was widowed, with a young daughter. She was unimpressed by Marilyn's voice which, she said, came over as 'a tight squeak when nervous.' (George Cukor was later to comment on Marilyn's 'quite unattractive' voice: her 'appealing baby voice,' he thought, was a very shrewd invention on her part.) Yet she was impressed by the girl's effort, her sense of hard work, her desire to succeed. As the relationship flourished, it is also likely that Natasha became quite infatuated with Marilyn. 'I breathed for her,' she once said. For the next seven years, until her dismissal, she devoted herself fanatically to her charge, being her dramatic coach on set on every film and thus braving the wrath of nearly all of Marilyn's directors, who were to include such intimidating gentlemen as Fritz Lang and Otto Preminger.

For her part, Marilyn seems to have had a strange need for what Arthur Miller called 'unstable older women.' As will be seen, Natasha was later to be superceded by Paula Strasberg, who was an even more bizarre character. At one time, too, Marilyn had quite a close friendship with Joan Crawford, partly through their mutual interest in Christian Science. There are differing versions why they eventually fell out. One claimed that Crawford made an unwelcome pass at Marilyn; another alleged that Marilyn took exception to some scathing remarks Crawford made about the way she flaunted herself on her public appearances. Marilyn's only public response to Crawford's criticism was: 'I've always admired her for being such a wonderful mother – for taking four children and giving them a fine home. Who better than I knows what that means to homeless little ones?' It is a curious remark. Was it her 'little girl lost' appeal for public sympathy? Was it meant purely ironically, Marilyn knowing what really went on behind the closed parental doors of Mommie Dearest? (Marilyn had a highly developed sense of irony, as witness her congratulations to Grace Kelly on hearing of her engagement to Prince Rainier of Monaco, who had first shown interest in

ABOVE: On the set of *Love Happy* in 1949, with Groucho Marx.

Marilyn as a possible wife: 'I'm so glad you've found a way out of this business'). Or was it more revealing than that – a suggestion that Marilyn's attraction to these women was a projection and idealization of her frustrating relationship with her mother?

Needless to say, for Natasha to function effectively as a drama coach, there must be some drama to begin with on which to work, and for a time such material proved elusive. Marilyn made an appearance in one scene in the Marx Brothers' comedy, *Love Happy* (1949), in which Groucho plays a private detective called Sam Grunion. 'Mr Grunion,' said Marilyn, 'I want you to help me . . . some men are following me.' To which Groucho inimitably replied: 'I can't imagine why.' One can almost see the eyebrows twitching. In the agreeable 1950 western musical, *A Ticket to Tomahawk*, yet again Marilyn played a rather dumb chorus girl who coos a lot in unison but does not have an individual line of dialogue. She played a decorative role in one of Dan Dailey's musical numbers, 'O What A Forward Young Man You Are,' almost causing him to fall over when he has to lift her in a dance routine; and she was given a piece of comic business during an Indian attack when she fires a gun with her eyes closed and still manages to hit something. But neither was the kind of part substantial enough to get a young actress noticed.

LEFT: A Marilyn pose from 1948.

RIGHT: An interesting glamour pic from 1950: an embryonic star about to burst from its shell.

RIGHT: Marilyn on the rocks in 1950.

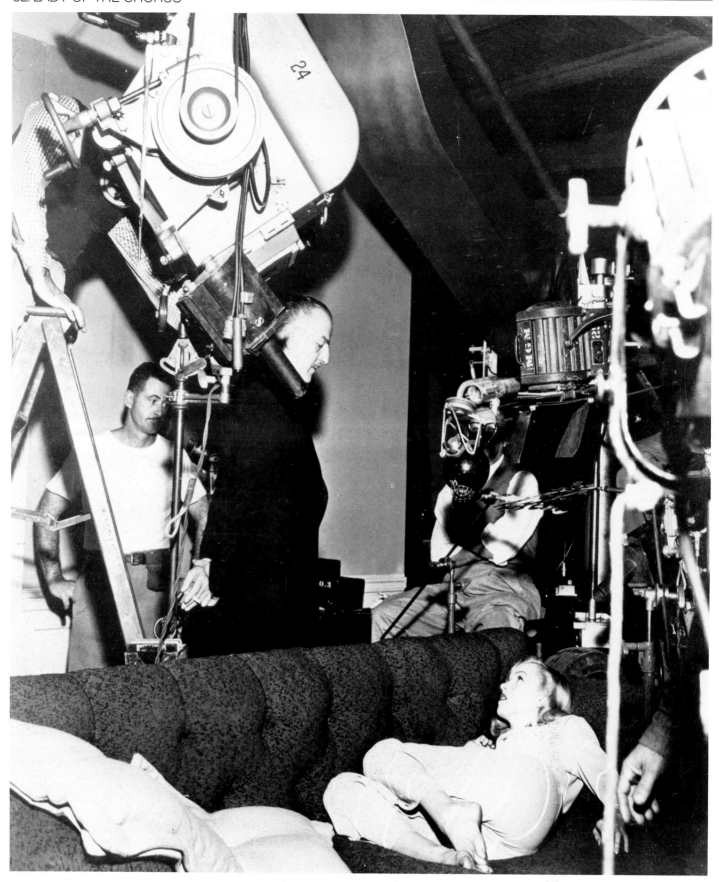

ABOVE: Shooting her first scene in *The Asphalt Jungle* (1950). Marilyn on the sofa; Louis Calhern (standing) as her 'uncle' Lon.

The first major break came with her role in John Huston's classic movie about a bank robbery, *The Asphalt Jungle* (1950). The credit for securing the role for Marilyn belongs entirely to the agent Johnny Hyde, a fast-talking diminutive man who had discovered Lana Turner, managed Rita Hayworth and, at the age of 53, met and fell in love with the 23-year-old Marilyn. Hyde's devotion to, and belief in her, both on a personal and professional level, was total. At the time he met Marilyn, he was sick with heart-disease, but he threw all his energies – and in so doing broke up his 20-year-old marriage – into promoting his young protegée. 'I am convinced that we would never have known the joy of Marilyn Monroe had it not been for an extraordinary agent named Johnny Hyde,' said playwright Garson Kanin, who was pestered by Hyde to let Marilyn play the lead in the film version of Kanin's *Born Yesterday* (1950) (the role was eventually to win Judy Holliday an Oscar). However, the decision was Harry Cohn's at Columbia and he would not hear of it. Undeterred, Hyde now lobbied John Huston, pushing Marilyn's claim for a small but crucial role in *The Asphalt Jungle* as the niece – Hollywood euphemism for mistress – of a crooked lawyer twice her age (Louis Calhern). 'Some sweet kid,' purrs Calhern in a tone that is far from avuncular.

Huston had originally cast Lola Albright in the role but, at Hyde's insistence and dimly remembering Marilyn as an attractive girl who had hung around the set of Huston's previous film for Columbia, *We Were Strangers* (1949), he tested Marilyn in the scene in which the character of Angela first appears. In the script, she is discovered asleep on the sofa but, as there was no sofa in the office, Marilyn asked if she could do the scene on the floor. Huston agreed and quickly sensed that she had the quality of sensuality and yet childlike innocence the part required. When Darryl Zanuck saw the film, he was enormously impressed by her and had to be told that Twentieth Century Fox had released her from her contract two years ago. 'For God's sake, get her back!' he bellowed and they did, on a new seven-year contract.

If Marilyn's contribution to *The Asphalt Jungle* remains memorable, it is partly because it is the most tender in a tough movie, and partly because of her acting in her last scene with Calhern, which she felt was one of the best things she ever did on film. Calhern is being interrogated by the police in his home, and Angela (Monroe) is now pressed by the chief inspector to say whether the alibi she provided for Calhern was the truth. She says, 'Yes,' while vigorously shaking her head and, 'No,' while vigorously nodding. She then breaks down, torn in two between a fear of self-incrimination and yet a genuine affection for Calhern and a distaste for informing on him. The dilemma of her character must have struck some uncomfortable chords at the time of HUAC when so many people were informing on their friends to save their own skin (at least four key personalities on the film were shortly to be arraigned by the Committee). Maybe Marilyn could bring such force to the scene because of her own confusion about the truths and falsehoods told about her own background in order for her to get ahead. When Calhern finally

LEFT: Marilyn as the 'niece' in *The Asphalt Jungle* (1950). Director John Huston told her: 'You could become a very good actress.'

BELOW: Searching for Hollywood sharks? A tentative toe in the water (1952).

ABOVE: The renowned party scene in *All About Eve* (1950). Chaperoned by George Sanders (right), Marilyn is introduced to a demure Anne Baxter (left) and a fearsome Bette Davis (second from left).

prompts her to tell the police the truth, she does so, and then takes his hand. 'I'm sorry, Uncle Lon,' she says, 'I tried . . . What about our trip, is it still on?' 'Don't worry, baby,' Calhern replies in a peculiar tone of sardonic sadness, 'you'll have plenty of trips.' It is the pay-off line, half grateful, half embittered, of an elderly man at the climax of his life saying farewell to this vision of beauty he has cherished and helped, and probably also corrupted. Similar farewells in real life were no doubt a regular part of Marilyn's experience during these years, as she flitted in and out of people's lives and homes ('like a flea on a griddle,' as her first agent, Harry Lipton said).

'Ah, Margo, you remember Miss Caswell,' purrs drama critic, Addison De Witt (George Sanders), introducing the beautiful blonde at his side to the party hostess, and grand actress, Margo Channing (Bette

Davis). 'I do not,' Margo snaps back, 'how do you do?' 'We've never met,' replies Miss Caswell (Marilyn Monroe), 'maybe that's why.' This was Marilyn's entrance in the classic with which she followed *The Asphalt Jungle*, Joseph L Mankiewicz's witty and wonderful study of theatrical bitchcraft, *All About Eve* (1950), which was to win the Oscar for the best film of 1950. Marilyn's opening riposte – artlessly naive but with a logic all its own – was to establish something of a comic trademark of hers, which she was to elaborate both on-screen and off. Cukor once said that her main trick in comedy was her manner of saying a funny line as if she did not quite see the joke, which made it funnier still. As the aspiring starlet, Miss Caswell in *All About Eve*, Marilyn is more the butt of the jokes than the deliverer of them. 'That's Max Fabian, the producer,' says De Witt to her, pointing her in the producer's direction, 'now go and do yourself some good.' Taking into account Mankiewicz's insider's relish for Hollywood gossip, one suspects that line might have been a specific satirical reference to Marilyn's relationship with either Joseph Schenck or Johnny Hyde.

Marilyn only appeared in two scenes in the film, but even so she seems to have made some impression on the distinguished cast. Her second short scene in a theater lobby required 25 takes, according to Gary Merrill, who played the director. For the party scene, she was an hour late, though given the fact that the scene requires all the stars to assemble together and to play characters with their claws unsheathed, it is not surprising that the scene was so terrifying and intimidating for a young actress. She comes through it very well.

Celeste Holm, who played the writer's wife and Margo's best friend (though ironically, Bette Davis in her autobiography says she could not stand the lady), rather disparagingly remembered what she called Marilyn's 'Betty Boop' quality. 'I thought she was quite sweet and terribly dumb,' said Miss Holm, 'and my natural reaction was "Whose girl was that?" It was the performance of a chorus girl.' This, of course, was precisely what the part required, and what De Witt means when he describes Miss Caswell as a 'graduate of the Copacabana School of Dramatic Art.' This, incidentally, might have been another of Mankiewicz's satirical shafts aimed at Marilyn's drama lessons. His memories of Monroe, apart from the incident already mentioned about the book of Rilke, are chiefly to do with his impression of her 'aloneness.' 'By which,' he says, 'I don't mean lonely: I mean the feeling she gave of being alone.'

Nearly all of Marilyn's lines are played to George Sanders who, in his autobiography, said he knew she was going to be a star because she *needed to*. He did not mention an incident some time before the film, when a very drunken George Sanders had sat next to Marilyn at a party, sized her up as 'blonde, pneumatic, full of peasant health. Just the type for me!,' proposed marriage, and then promptly fallen asleep. After *All About Eve*, Marilyn did not see him again until another party two years later when he was escorting his new bride Zsa Zsa Gabor – equally blonde, pneumatic and full of peasant health – whom Marilyn acidly described as 'one of those blondes who put on ten years if you take a close look at them.'

This was the start of a very busy period for Marilyn, in which little by little she was inching her way further into the public eye. The majority of the movies she made between 1950 and 1952 were not particularly distinguished, but they came regularly – she made ten in two years – and made her known. If she was refining her dramatic art in the process, Johnny Hyde ensured that her physical appearance was brought as near to perfection as modern surgery could achieve. Fred Karger had arranged for a dentist to fix her uneven teeth. Now, under the supervision of Johnny Hyde, hairdressers were hired to bleach her hair regularly; her nose was lifted slightly; and some cartilage was placed in her jaw to strengthen the profile of her chin line. Hyde's obsessive efforts on her behalf took their toll on his already frail health and he died of a heart attack on 18 December 1950. Despite entreaties by the family, who saw Marilyn as a 'homewrecker,' to stay away from the funeral, Marilyn attended and, according to witnesses, threw herself on the coffin.

BELOW: Marilyn wins a beauty contest in the 1952 comedy, *We're Not Married*.

ABOVE: Marilyn's glamorous secretary takes years off her boss, Albert Dekker, in the 1951 film, *As Young as You Feel*.

Many have suggested that Marilyn's relationship with Hyde was entirely in the interests of her own career. Yet there are at least three definitive refutations of that. In his book, *Hollywood*, Garson Kanin recalled her telling him that 'I had plenty of friends and acquaintances – you know what I mean, acquaintances? And sure, I played the game the way everyone else was playing it. But not one of them, not one of those big shots, ever did a damn thing for me, not one, except Johnny. Because he believed in me. He was the first kind man I met in my whole life.' Kanin did not doubt that she was genuine. Arthur Miller remembered being introduced to Marilyn for the first time by Elia Kazan in her dressing room and discovering her with her eyes swollen with tears: afterwards he learned that she had just heard of Hyde's death. And, if her liaison with Hyde had simply been an opportunistic career move, her action a week after his death is even more inex-

plicable: she attempted suicide by stuffing her mouth with a bottle-full of sleeping pills. Natasha Lytess found a note from Marilyn, leaving 'my car and fur stole to Natasha,' and another note on her daughter's bedroom door exhorting the reader of it to ensure that Natasha's daughter did not enter the room. When Natasha rushed in, she found a half-dressed Marilyn, barely conscious, with cheeks 'puffed out like an adder's' said Natasha, and a mouth full of a wet greenish substance she had not yet swallowed. Natasha's arrival home was unexpected and death was only narrowly averted.

It would be pointless to enumerate all of the films she made during this two-year period, since not even the presence of Marilyn can make some of them of any interest. One of the more notable was *As Young as You Feel* (1951), in which Marilyn, as she did so often, played the boss's secretary. She did little but walk-throughs but was so

good that her co-star, Constance Bennett, remarked: 'There's a broad with a future behind her.' The movie was based on a story by Paddy Chayefsky, who was later to write *The Goddess* (1958), the tragic story of a Monroe type heroine, played by Kim Stanley, and a pungent and prophetic critique of what Hollywood and the Monroe cult was doing to its star.

Love Nest (1951) and *Let's Make It Legal* (1951) were two mild comedies that showed off Marilyn's beauty and were scripted by I A L Diamond, who was later to collaborate with Billy Wilder on indubitably the greatest comedy of Marilyn's career, *Some Like It Hot* (1959). In the portmanteau film, *O. Henry's Full House* (1952), she had the delicious opportunity of playing a streetwalker opposite Charles Laughton's bum; and in Fritz Lang's excellent *Clash by Night* (1952) she made a big impression playing Barbara Stanwyck's sister-in-law who envies the older woman's apparent freedom.

ABOVE: In *Let's Make It Legal* (1951), Marilyn, not for the first time, played a gold-digging blonde. Here she is seen with Macdonald Carey (left), Zachary Scott (second from right), and Claudette Colbert (right).

LEFT: Marilyn with her co-star Keith Andes in Fritz Lang's *Clash by Night* (1952). One critic commented: 'Miss Monroe even looks alluring in blue jeans.'

In Howard Hawks's superb screwball comedy, *Monkey Business* (1952), she played Miss Laurel, secretary to Charles Coburn, who after trying and failing to teach her the rudiments of typing and watching her wiggling exit, comments consolingly: 'Anyone can type.' She also attracts the attention of Cary Grant's absent-minded professor, who has developed a drug aimed at restoring people's youth but which succeeds in subversively regressing them to childhood. 'She's half-infant,' says Grant of Monroe to his jealous wife Ginger Rogers, who snaps back: 'Not the half that's visible.' It is a role which comically, but also disturbingly, combines Monroe's twin assets of sweet child-woman and fearsomely formidable sexual creature. The critic Robin Wood referred to her 'half-infant' character as 'an example of fully-developed immaturity,' while the French critic, and later filmmaker, Jacques Rivette referred to Monroe in this film as 'that monster of femininity whom the costume designer nearly deformed.'

The so-called comic contrast between the mind of a child and the spectacular body of a woman was the predominant feature of nearly all Marilyn's roles at this time. In 1951 her dissatisfaction at this situation was highlighted and intensified when, on the recommendation of her actor friend Jack Palance, Marilyn enrolled in the acting classes of Michael Chekhov. Chekhov was the nephew of the great Russian dramatist, Anton Chekhov, and a student of Stanislavsky. He is probably best known for his classic text on acting, *To The Actor*, and for his Oscar-nominated performance as Ingrid Bergman's psychiatrist friend in Hitchcock's *Spellbound* (1945), who, in one of Ben Hecht's wittiest lines, bids her 'good night, and sweet dreams – which we will analyze at breakfast.' Chekhov became another of those hero-cum-psychiatrist-cum-father figures who she was to cherish all her life. One of her presents to him, an engraving of Lincoln, had the inscription: 'Lincoln was the man I admired most of all through school. Now that man is you.' (Coincidentally, Arthur Miller's first present to Marilyn was to be Carl Sandburg's biography of Lincoln. 'American Presidents' is another curious thread that ran consistently through her life.)

For his part, Chekhov was delighted with her, even when she arrived late and sent poignant notes, acknowledging that she 'tried his patience' and yet needed 'his friendship desperately.' In one session, she played Cordelia to his King Lear and she was, according to Chekhov, 'mesmerizing.' At another session, when rehearsing a

scene from Anton Chekhov's *The Cherry Orchard*, Chekhov remarked that Marilyn was giving off powerful sexual vibrations, which Marilyn said were completely unconscious. 'I understand your problem with the studio now, Marilyn,' he said, 'and why they refuse to regard you as an actress. You are more valuable to them as a sex stimulant.'

The major exception to this stereotype of Marilyn during these years and the first opportunity she had to give an indication of her ability as a dramatic actress, came in the film, *Don't Bother To Knock* (1952), directed by Roy Baker from a screenplay by Daniel Taradash and in which Marilyn played a psychopathic baby-sitter. The film was not a commercial success and had mixed reviews, most critics preferring Monroe as the 'dumb blonde.' Yet Anne Bancroft, her co-star, has said that she was tremendously

ABOVE: With Cary Grant during the making of *Monkey Business* in 1952.

FAR LEFT: 'I have something to show you': Marilyn shows Cary Grant the new acetate stockings he has invented in *Monkey Business*.

impressed by her, particularly in the scene where Bancroft has to disarm this disturbed creature who is preparing to kill herself with a razor blade. 'There was just this scene of one woman seeing another woman who was helpless and in pain,' said Bancroft to an interviewer, 'and she *was* helpless and in pain. It was so real, I responded . . . she moved me so, tears came into my eyes. Believe me, such moments happened rarely.' It is probable that in this scene, which Marilyn herself thought was one of her best, she was drawing on her own disturbed childhood, using her past and her pain – in other words, instinctively applying the Method a good two years before she set foot inside The Actors' Studio. The conflict between Marilyn's ambitions and gifts as an actress and her commercial value as a sex symbol was to be the source of numerous disputes between Marilyn and Twentieth Century Fox in the coming years.

This conflict, however, was deferred because of a remarkable controversy involv-ing Marilyn early in 1952. One of the draw-backs of mounting celebrity is that it seems to prompt an unpleasant sound – the rattle of skeletons in the family cupboard. Marilyn certainly had two such skeletons that began rattling as her fame grew: there may have been three. One was the fate of her mother who, contrary to early publicity, was found to be not dead but mad and in a state mental hospital. The mini-crisis was deftly dealt with by the portrayal of Marilyn as a sensi-tive, caring daughter. A second skeleton was her alleged marriage in Mexico to a young writer she had met years before at Fox, Bob Slatzer in 1952. According to Slatzer, the marriage lasted three days but the studio put a stop to it, instructing the couple to bribe the lawyer to destroy the marriage certificate. The story never reached public circulation. The third skele-ton received world-wide coverage and was an exposure of a very literal kind.

The embarrassing revelation was, of course, the discovery that in 1949 Fox's new

FAR RIGHT: With Richard Widmark in *Don't Bother to Knock* (1952).

RIGHT: A sultry Marilyn in 1952. Her Rita Hayworth look?

LEFT: Marilyn as the star attraction in the Grand Marshal parade in Atlantic City in 1952.

BELOW: High spirits: Marilyn on location in Canada for *River Of No Return* (1954).

starlet had posed in the nude for photographer Tom Kelley who had paid Marilyn $50 and sold the photographs for a calendar series. Nowadays it is difficult to imagine those innocent times in which such a discovery could scandalize a nation and ruin a career. It has been suggested that it was a deliberate publicity stunt, though considering the risk involved in calculating public opinion, this seems unlikely. At first the studio was inclined to deny it but faced with the inescapable evidence and with Marilyn's agreement, Twentieth Century Fox decided instead to make light of it and tell the truth to the world as charmingly as possible.

The story went that Marilyn had only agreed to pose for the pictures (relatively mild shots of her lying nude on a crumpled red velvet carpet) because she needed the money to reclaim her secondhand car that had been re-possessed by the finance company when she failed to keep up payments. This was a plausible enough story. William Holden has the same predicament in *Sunset Boulevard* (1950), claiming: 'If I lose my car, I lose my legs.' Arthur Miller could even remember writing a poem on the theme that 'An actress can't succeed in Hollywood without a car.'

Nevertheless, it is probable that Marilyn's contrition was somewhat exaggerated. She was never exactly embarrassed by nudity; once even did an interview completely naked; and wanted to appear nude in a scene in *The Misfits* (1961) (which she does, visibly startling Clark Gable, but the audience sees only her bare back). But her honesty disarmed the press, and the wit with which she parried the most obvious awkward questions – whether of her own invention or that of an astute press agent – turned a potentially disastrous affair into something of a personal triumph. 'Did you have *anything* on?' she was asked. 'Oh yes,' she would reply, 'the radio'; or, as a variation, 'Chanel No. 5.' In a year's time, the magazine *Playboy* was to launch its first edition with Marilyn's nude pose as its first centerfold, symbolizing its philosophy: where sex is related not to sickness, shame and guilt but 'to happiness, to beauty, to health and to feelings of pleasure and fulfillment.' By that time her career was fully launched, and the obscure calendar girl was the world's foremost film star.

FAR RIGHT: The calendar pose that shook a nation: Marilyn as America's most notorious nude.

BELOW: The commercial exploitation of Marilyn's notoriety.

Chapter Three

'AFTER YOU GET WHAT YOU WANT, YOU DON'T WANT IT'

Marilyn As Star (1953-1955)

'I have loved her since *Niagara* and even before. She is a person of grace, somewhere between Chaplin and James Dean. How could anyone resist a film that has Marilyn Monroe in it?' FRANÇOIS TRUFFAUT

Securing recognition is one thing: dealing with it is quite another. To begin with, stardom must have seemed for Marilyn the fulfillment of a dream and, in a way, it was. From out of the shadows of a horrific childhood, she had created a new world for herself, a new *persona* – or so she thought. But Marilyn was never quite able to escape the trauma of having once been Norma Jeane: it is possibly this nagging anxiety behind the allure that added to her fascination in the public's eyes. Harlow amuses, and Garbo inspires awe, but Marilyn elicits affection, because of her innocence and vulnerability. As early as 1953, in *Niagara*, the critic Gavin Lambert was noting that Marilyn seemed too frightened to be a vamp and that for all her pin-up smile at the attention she attracts, there was something oddly mournful about her, as if she had just woken up from a bad dream. It was an astute observation. When personal and professional problems began to build up in the late 1950s, so her old fears and insecurities re-emerged in a new form. 'Celebrity,' as Arthur Miller has observed, 'is merely a different form of loneliness.'

On the surface, her career was flourishing. Between 1953 and 1955, she appeared in six films, not one of which was great but all of which were successful and in all of which Marilyn was the primary reason for what success and quality they had. The first of these was Henry Hathaway's flamboyant melodrama, *Niagara* (1953), in which Marilyn played a villainess attempting to provoke an infatuated young man into murdering her deranged husband (Joseph Cotten). Ostensibly the most unsympathetic role of her career, her sexuality seeming entirely destructive, Marilyn gave the character an intriguing undertone of desperation and certainly an erotic potency, which made the other law-abiding characters seem positively bloodless by comparison. The film is particularly remembered today for its poster, in which Marilyn upstages the Niagara Falls as a symbol of tempestuous romance; and for Marilyn's first appearance, a protracted shot of her as she undulates away

LEFT: Competing romantic attractions: Marilyn poses against the background of the Niagara Falls.

FAR LEFT: Marilyn in 1957; always the perfect model, even during her most serious acting period.

from the camera in high heels and a tight red dress that must rank as one of the most striking entrances in reverse in Hollywood history. When the film's symbol of female normality, Jean Peters, is asked by her husband why she does not wear clothes like that, she replies: 'You have to start laying your plans at 13 for a dress like that.'

Niagara was followed by Howard Hawks's brash musical-comedy *Gentlemen Prefer Blondes* (1953), in which Marilyn was teamed up with Jane Russell to launch a fearsome female assault – blonde and brunette, greed and lust – on a petrified man's world. Described by Hawks as a 'travesty on sex,' the film has tended to divide critics. They cannot agree on whether it is a celebration or send-up of sexism, the confusion only compounded by the final romantic conclusion ('the pairing of Marilyn Monroe and Jane Russell with Tommy Noonan and Elliott Reid,' commented the critic Richard Corliss, 'may well be the most ill-suited in American films'). Some commentators felt that Marilyn's innocent *persona* was at odds with a character for whom diamonds are a girl's best friend ('square cut or pear-shaped/those rocks won't lost *their* shape . . .'). However, it must be said that the authoress of the original book, Anita Loos,

thought that 'Marilyn *was* Lorelei Lee, I knew she'd be perfect in it.' Similarly delighted was Darryl Zanuck, who had no idea of Marilyn's vocal skills and, on first seeing the film, thought she had been dubbed.

As befitted their relationship in the film, Marilyn and Jane Russell got on extremely well together. Their most publicized appearance during the shooting was at the famous ceremony outside Grauman's Theater in Los Angeles, where the screen immortals put their hands and feet in wet cement on the pavement. It was Marilyn who suggested that, in their case, it might be more appropriate if Jane put her bosom in the cement and Marilyn her behind. The only source of friction between them was not personal but had to do with Marilyn's studio contract. If gentlemen preferred blondes, she thought, why was she receiving only about a tenth of the salary of her brunette co-star? It was an omen of several such arguments that were brewing between Marilyn and Twentieth Century Fox.

It is also true that, although he directed her in two films (and, according to Billy Wilder later, any director who survived that experience ought to be awarded a Purple Heart, if not an Oscar), Marilyn never really

BELOW and RIGHT: Femininity at its most formidable: Marilyn with Jane Russell in *Gentlemen Prefer Blondes* (1953).

ABOVE: Marilyn's foot and handprints outside Grauman's Chinese Theater, the ceremony originally performed at the time of the premiere of *Gentlemen Prefer Blondes* in June 1953. The floral tribute was placed there by the management of the Theater after Marilyn's death.

LEFT: Glamour Queen: Marilyn in 1952.

BELOW: Nice and easy: Marilyn luxuriates on a couch in 1957.

RIGHT: Marilyn in *Niagara* (1953).

got on with Howard Hawks. To be fair, she never played the kind of heroine who interested Hawks – she was passive rather than active, and innocent rather than ironic. Describing her in an interview as 'a frightened girl' who 'never felt she was good enough to do the things she did,' Hawks gave an insight into the kind of fears and crises of self-confidence that were to manifest themselves in alarming forms in later years. 'We had a lot of fun doing *Gentlemen Prefer Blondes*,' he said, 'but there were a lot of times when I was ready to give up the ghost. Jane Russell would say, ''Look at me – all he wants you to do is such a thing,'' and Marilyn would say, ''Why didn't you tell me?'' Very strange girl . . . She'd sit around on the set and nobody'd pay any attention to her . . . yet she had this strange effect when photographed.'

Her third big hit of 1953 was *How to Marry a Millionaire*, the first Cinemascope comedy. It is about three friends who rent a penthouse to ensnare some eligible wealthy men. Marilyn's co-stars were the formidable Lauren Bacall and Betty Grable, but again it is Marilyn who steals the show as a myopic manhunter who, for reasons of vanity, is often shedding her enormous spectacles and consequently reading books upside down and walking into walls. The writer

LEFT: A myopic Marilyn finds out how to marry a millionaire. With Betty Grable (right).

BELOW: Marilyn with her co-stars in *How To Marry A Millionaire*: Lauren Bacall (center) and Betty Grable (right).

BELOW: Marilyn with actors Rory Calhoun (who plays her gambling husband) and Tommy Rettig (the boy) in *River of No Return* (1954). Robert Mitchum is soon to replace Calhoun in her affections.

Nunnally Johnson was probably right in saying of her role, 'that it was the first time anybody genuinely liked Marilyn for herself . . . she herself said it was the only picture she had been in in which she had a measure of modesty.' For the second time in her career, the first being in *We're Not Married*, (1952), she wound up with David Wayne as her husband – a fine actor but hardly the most handsome leading man for the screen's foremost sex symbol.

Recollecting working with Marilyn, Lauren Bacall remembered that Betty Grable was very kind to her, recognizing that her own reign as blonde movie queen was now over and that this new contender was about to replace her. Although she liked Marilyn, Bacall found her difficult to act with, because she had the habit of focusing on your forehead rather than looking you in the eyes. The reason for this was that she was probably searching for a signal of approval from her dramatic coach, Natasha Lytess, who was now a constant – and for Marilyn a necessary – presence on the set.

Like Howard Hawks, director Jean Negulesco was somewhat taken aback by Marilyn's minimal self-confidence. She had approached him with all kinds of anxieties about her role and suggestions about how to approach them. 'Marilyn,' he told her,

'the only motivation you need for this part is the fact that in this movie you are as blind as a bat without glasses.' He was even more taken aback during shooting, when a small scene, in which she has breakfast in bed and has to take a phone call, was still not finished after a day of shooting. Sometimes she would answer the phone before it had rung; at others, she would drink out of a cup before it had any coffee in it. Negulesco retired exhausted. 'We'll do it in the morning, honey, don't worry about it,' said Nunnally Johnson, to which Marilyn replied: 'Don't worry about what?'

In *River of No Return* (1954), shot mainly on location in Canada, she had a strong co-star, Robert Mitchum, and an equally forceful, not to say tyrannical director, Otto Preminger. In the film, Marilyn played a saloon girl who becomes involved with an ex-prisoner (Mitchum) and his son (Tommy Rettig). Within a melodramatic plot-line involving murder, double-cross, roaring rapids, and marauding Indians, there beats a rather thoughtful movie about a conflict between two contrasting attitudes to life – one stiff and unyielding (Mitchum), the other impulsive and unstable (Monroe). Caught in between is the young boy whom they both love. The river is also symbolic of their characters: Mitchum tries to master it,

RIGHT: Marilyn shows off her injured ankle, hurt during the filming of *River of No Return*. The sly look on her face suggests it might not be as bad as she is making out.

BELOW: As the saloon singer in *River of No Return*.

FAR RIGHT: A picture of Marilyn taken in 1954 at the Baron Studios.

Monroe is content to drift along wherever it takes her. The title song expresses this well, and Marilyn sings it in a wistful tone of resignation and regret that she will scarcely equal until her rendering of 'I'm Through With Love' in *Some Like It Hot* (1959).

Mitchum and Marilyn were good friends, but the filming was not a happy occasion. Early on Marilyn, who usually got on well with children, was puzzled by the coolness towards her of Tommy Rettig, who is probably best remembered today as the young hero of the cult classic, *The Five Thousand Fingers of Dr T* (1953). It emerged that, because of Marilyn's lurid reputation after the nude calendar incident, young Rettig had been forced to seek permission from his priest even to appear in this film – and was consequently still very wary. Later Natasha Lytess got to Rettig, reducing him to tears by telling him that all child actors lose their

talent by the time they are 14, and an enraged Preminger banned her from the set . (As it happened, Natasha was right about Rettig, an accomplished child actor who never made it into adult roles and ended up in federal prison for smuggling cocaine.) In retaliation against Preminger, Marilyn sustained a leg injury during a hazardous stunt which delayed production. The leg injury was almost certainly faked, since Shelley Winters remembers going to a dance with Marilyn on the night after she was supposed to have broken it. 'Dumb blonde indeed,' said Winters, 'like a fox was my young friend Marilyn.'

Marilyn's rebellion during the shooting of *River of No Return* began to extend to her relationship with the studio. Because of her dissatisfaction with the script, she turned down *The Girl in Pink Tights*, even though it would have meant co-starring with one of her favorite male stars, Frank Sinatra (incidentally, the film was then never made). She tried and failed to land the role of Sinatra's girl-friend, Adelaide in Joseph L Mankiewicz's film of *Guys and Dolls* (1955) – Mankiewicz insisted that the role go to the actress who played the part on stage, Vivian Blaine. As a compromise, she agreed to appear in a film she did not want to do if the studio would guarantee her the leading role in a film she wanted to do very much. The movie she did not particularly like was the lackluster tribute to Irving Berlin, *There's No Business Like Show Business* (1954), in which Marilyn had a comparatively small role and two reasonable musical numbers,

'Heat Wave' and 'After You Get What You Want, You Don't Want It.' The film she did want – and her performance fully justified her enthusiasm – was Billy Wilder's *The Seven-Year Itch* (1955).

Based on George Axelrod's hugely successful Broadway play, *The Seven-Year Itch* tells the story of a middle-aged New Yorker (Tom Ewell). Left alone in his apartment when his wife and children go off on holiday, he is tempted by the prospect of an affair with the girl upstairs (Marilyn Monroe), the two having previously met when she narrowly missed accidentally dropping a plant-pot on his head. It is a satire on movie romances, notably David Lean's *Brief Encounter* (1945) and Fred Zinnemann's *From Here to Eternity* (1953), and on American sexual behavior in the post-Kinsey Report era. Marilyn's performance as the Colorado model and TV commercials 'actress' is her most exuberant. Although the play belonged to the man, in the film the comic highlights are nearly all Marilyn's, like her comment on being able to recognize classical music 'because it has no vocal,' or her calm reaction to the hero's abject apology after his failed seduction: 'Oh it hap-

ABOVE: Marilyn performs 'Lazy' with Donald O'Connor (left) and Mitzi Gaynor (right). From *There's No Business Like Show Business* (1954).

RIGHT: 'Not only is there no God,' said Woody Allen, 'try getting a plumber at weekends.' Yet Marilyn has no trouble in *The Seven-Year Itch* (1955), when she gets her big toe stuck while taking a bath.

pens to me all the time.' It was a performance that in Billy Wilder's words, 'had flesh impact . . . when she was on the screen there was never a hole' but it is also a performance of an immensely good-natured charm that somehow transcends sex. This is even true of the most famous shot in her screen career: the moment when she stands over a subway grating and allows the breeze from the train below to blow her skirt above her waist. As memorable as the erotic impact of the image is the look of girlish joy on her face.

Nothing is more characteristic of the typical turbulence of Marilyn's life than the fact that this zenith of her public popularity simultaneously marked a nadir in her private life. It seems generally agreed that it was this particular scene in *The Seven-Year Itch*, and the public pandemonium that accompanied its shooting, that marked the end of her marriage to Joe DiMaggio, which had begun only nine months previously. He had been increasingly alenated by her stardom and shocked by the immodest, exhibitionist nature of the roles she was called upon to play. Marilyn had first met DiMaggio on a blind date in 1952. By all accounts,

LEFT: A studio shot of Marilyn as she prepares for the skirt-billowing shot in *The Seven-Year Itch* (1955).

BELOW: Marilyn's magic moment in *The Seven-Year Itch*, watched by her co-star, Tom Ewell.

existent and his reading confined to comics and the sports pages. It also seems likely that DiMaggio underestimated the strain that Marilyn's stardom would put on their relationship. He thought he had acquired a wife: he found he had actually acquired a public property. Even their honeymoon had to be interrupted when Marilyn was prevailed upon to untertake a morale-boosting tour of Korea for UN troops.

far from being awed by the man's un-equalled baseball prowess that had made him a national hero prior to his retirement in 1951, Marilyn, who was no sports fan, had barely heard of him. Nevertheless, he impressed her as a quiet, dignified, old-fashioned man who treated ladies with courtesy and consideration. The romance blossomed, yet it was not without some trepidation that Marilyn finallly agreed to get married on 14 January 1954.

Various reasons have been put forward for the marital breakdown. In many ways they were incompatible. DiMaggio was fastidious whereas Marilyn was compulsively untidy. They shared very few interests. Marilyn, who by this time was earnestly endeavoring to improve herself educationally, was exasperated by the fact that DiMaggio's intellectual conversation was non-

This might not have been so bad if she had not enjoyed herself so much. 'The highlight of my life,' she was to call it. One of her numbers, 'Do it Again' had to be banned for fear it might cause a riot. On another occasion, her famous remark to 10,000 men at a US marine base – 'I don't know why you boys are always getting so excited over sweater girls; take away their sweaters and what have they got?' – did cause a riot. Contrary to her screen image, Marilyn knew precisely the effect she was having on the opposite sex, and she was revelling in it. DiMaggio was undoubtedly appalled.

Jealousy seems to have been a large factor in their eventual parting. During the period when she was being officially courted by DiMaggio, she seems to have continued having affairs with other men. It was during this period that her second mar-

BELOW: Entertaining the troops in Korea – and how! Marilyn interrupted her honeymoon for this tour.

riage to Bob Slatzer is alleged to have taken place. Another lover of hers at this time, according to some witnesses, was Edward G Robinson Jr, an aspiring actor tragically unable to step out of the shadow of his father and whose only noted film-role was as the coin-tossing gangster in *Some Like It Hot* (1959) who emerges out of a birthday cake to machine-gun Spats Columbo and his gang. Evidence suggested that it might have been Robinson Jr who first introduced Marilyn to drugs.

It should be stressed perhaps that, although only those affairs of Marilyn have been mentioned in which there is corrob-orative evidence, there is still a good deal of hearsay about Marilyn's sexual behavior at this time. For the most part, any affairs of hers during this period seem to have been short-lived, casual and friendly. An excep-tion was her relationship with her vocal coach, Hal Schaefer, during the making of *There's No Business Like Show Business* (1954). The harassment of Schaefer by DiMaggio's friends, because of his relation-ship with Marilyn, ultimately led to Schaef-er's attempted suicide. In one particular in-cident, a DiMaggio war-party, led by Frank Sinatra, had launched a raid on the man's apartment, clearly intending violence. It was fortunate for everyone concerned that they got the wrong apartment.

Allegations were made at the time about DiMaggio's physical violence towards Marilyn. Yet there is no doubt that the split-up when it came was a difficult and

painful one for them both. No one who has seen the famous piece of newsreel of Mari-lyn as she leaves the press conference after her divorce announcement, pursued by a pack of newsmen, 'like animals at the kill,' can possibly forget the look of genuine grief on her tear-stained face. One other fact must be emphasized. At the time of her greatest need, after the break-up of her mar-riage with Arthur Miller and in the days and weeks both before and even after her death, DiMaggio proved her most devoted and loyal friend. Those who genuinely loved her never fell out of love with her – in spite of everything.

One of the ironies of her break-up with DiMaggio was that, just as he found the roles she played an intolerable public spec-tacle, Marilyn herself was becoming tired of the nature of the parts she was being offered. They seemed to break down into two very narrow categories: gold-digger or showgirls, or, just occasionally, gold-dig-ging showgirls. Even under the guidance of distinguished directors in the future, she was never really to break free of this, but certainly part of her argument with Twen-tieth Century Fox at this time was to do with their rigid stereotyping of her image. She was sold and adored as a sex symbol, the most desirable of dumb blondes, when Marilyn's desire at this time was to be re-spected as a serious actress and as a serious lady.

The precise reason for her professional problems, though, has been less remarked on than the symptoms of these problems: notably, her lateness and her inability to re-member lines. By now her reputation for this was becoming legendary. Billy Wilder, who said 'she has breasts like granite and a brain like Swiss cheese, full of holes,' became par-

TOP RIGHT: Signing the divorce papers on 27 October 1954. On Marilyn's left is her attorney, Jerry Giesler.

BELOW: Still friends: with DiMaggio at the premiere of *The Seven-Year Itch* in 1955.

ticularly aware of it while filming *The Seven-Year Itch* in 1954. He felt that the problem might not have been unique to Marilyn but had been aggravated by the fact that she was brought up at Fox, the Cinemascope studio. 'In Cinemascope you have to remember more than one line because you cannot cut – the screen is too wide – and therefore you cannot cheat,' said Wilder. 'You have to sustain a scene and have to learn the dialogue. She was completely unaware of her lack of training and inadequacies. . .'

Her lateness was equally trying. When she arrived late on *The Seven-Year Itch* set one day, she told Wilder it was because she 'couldn't find the studio.' 'This was the studio she'd been coming to for years,' commented Wilder. 'I was here mentally at nine,' she told Howard Hawks when she arrived at 10am for a 9am call. Her publicist and friend at Twentieth Century Fox, Roy Craft, remembered her buying a daily diary to help her with this problem but then noticing it was for the wrong year. The only major occasion when anyone could remember her arriving on time was the famous reception in Hollywood for Soviet Premier Kruschev. Billy Wilder was thunderstruck. 'That's it,' he said, 'Kruschev should direct all her movies.'

Yet why was Marilyn like this? Was it a ploy, a feminine tease to increase expectation? Or, more likely, was it a sort of distress signal, a symptom of helpless insecurity? One would guess that it was a combination of one-fifth narcissism and four-fifths stark terror.

The manufactured nature of Marilyn's glamour should be mentioned in this regard. It was not something that came naturally or was instinctive. Indeed, away from the sound-stage, Marilyn could be literally unrecognizable. There is a famous story about the rehearsal period for *The Prince and the Showgirl* (1957), when Dame Sybil Thorndike commented: 'She's awfully sweet this girl, but when's Marilyn coming?' She had to be told that it was Marilyn. It sounds implausible yet there are countless other stories of people not recognizing her in the flesh. Only at the moment of shooting did she become Marilyn, and it was a moment and a spark that had to be painstakingly recreated day after day. Each day she had to feel herself back into the role of Marilyn Monroe, a process that physically took at least three hours ('I know,' said Simone Signoret, 'because I watched it day after day'). The process was probably lengthened by the fact that Marilyn was feeling also that this sexy, glamorous *persona* was an increasingly burdensome role to sustain.

The stronger element was fear. Soundstage fright, one might call it. Of her directors, Hawks, Lang and Preminger all mentioned it. A wardrobe assistant said that Marilyn 'never felt secure in front of the cameras. She was so scared about looking right, acting right, that she was physically unable to leave the trailer.' Henry Weinstein, who was the producer on Marilyn's aborted final project, *Something's Got To Give*, said: 'Very few people experience terror. We all experience anxiety, unhappiness, heartbreak, but what Marilyn had was sheer primal terror.' One can only assume that such terror was rooted in a childhood insecurity that stardom – its transience, its responsibility, its incessant public inspection – magnified to a massive degree.

In this respect, Marilyn's next career move seemed eminently sensible. It involved being possibly less of a star and certainly more of an actress. It involved leaving Los Angeles for New York. It was not only a career move. She was once again in love.

BELOW: Marilyn escorted by Marlon Brando in 1955, a period in which they had a brief affair.

Chapter Four

METHOD IN HER MAGIC

Marilyn As Actress (1956-1959)

'Honey, just think of Coca-Cola and Frank Sinatra.'
PAULA STRASBERG

The Seven-Year Itch (1955) marked the end of what her friend Roy Craft was to call Marilyn's 'five *happy* years' at Fox. It did not represent her peak as a comedienne (that was to be touched in *Some Like It Hot* [1959]); nor was it her greatest moment as an actress (depending on individual preference, that would be either *Bus Stop* [1956] or *The Misfits* [1961]); but it was undoubtedly her high-point as star. Her most prodigious dramatic achievements lay ahead, but so did her most titanic personal and professional problems. She was never out of the headlines but, from now on, these tended to consist of medical bulletins as much as movie gossip.

On 1 January 1955, Marilyn had surprised the film world by forming her own production company in association with Milton Greene, who had formerly been a photographer for *Look* magazine. The two had met when Marilyn was one of his photographic assignments. 'Why, you're just a boy,' she said on first seeing him, to which Greene slowly replied, 'and you're just a girl,' and the two became instant friends. In conversation it became clear that Greene had ambitions to be a film producer. These ambitions quickly became connected to Marilyn's dissatisfaction with her roles at Twentieth Century Fox and also her contract, which she felt did not sufficiently reward her star status, either financially or artistically. Her situation with the studio was further inflamed when she turned down another project, *How To Be Very, Very Popular*, which made her very, very unpopular with Darryl Zanuck. (The film was subsequently made in 1955 without Marilyn and singularly failed to justify its title.)

The eventual outcome was a new contract, which gave her more money ($100,000 per film), director approval, and a commitment to do just four films for Fox over the next seven years. Things seemed to be working out according to Marilyn's design. However, her partnership with Greene proved to be unfortunately brief – it did not survive the traumatic experience of *The Prince and the Showgirl* (1957) – and the nature of Marilyn's roles was to remain relatively unchanged until her untimely death, although her interpretation of them undoubtedly deepened.

FAR LEFT: Philippe Halsman's shot for *Life* magazine, 1959.

BELOW: Marilyn as photographed by Milton Greene in 1956. *Time* magazine said: 'Always there was that traffic-jamming hunk of a woman that this scared little girl inhabited . . . What she needed . . . was not success but salvation.'

ABOVE: Publicizing *Baby Doll* on behalf of The Actors' Studio.

A significant factor towards the increasing complexity of her performances was her attendance at the legendary Actors' Studio in New York, home of the Method. The Studio was the theatrical laboratory of its co-founders Elia Kazan and Lee Strasberg and brought forth such graduates as Marlon Brando and Montgomery Clift. Marilyn had started attending in 1954 when The Studio was run by Lee Strasberg who, two decades later, would become known to a new generation of filmgoers through his magnificent performance as the subtly malevolent Mafia boss, Hyman Roth in Francis Ford Coppola's *The Godfather Part II* (1974). In the early sessions, Marilyn sat shyly at the back in dark glasses and, when asked to comment, said hesitantly: 'I just wanted to say – it was just like life.' She was quickly befriended by actors Eli Wallach and Kevin McCarthy, both of whom were later to appear with her in *The Misfits* (1961); and she was more or less adopted by Lee Strasberg and his wife, Paula, who become another of Marilyn's surrogate families.

There was one immediate and dramatic

consequence of this. Because she no longer had the qualifications to advise on Marilyn's new acting needs and philosophy, Natasha Lytess was fired as dramatic coach and replaced by Paula Strasberg. Natasha was devastated. 'Marilyn needs me like a dead man needs a coffin!' she wailed before returning broken-hearted to Europe.

There was probably some suspicion of Marilyn's attendance at The Studio, since Hollywood and the star system were the antithesis of what many thought The Actors' Studio should stand for. Hollywood was commerce; The Studio was art. Yet Marilyn and Strasberg were probably shrewdly recognizing and servicing each other's needs. Marilyn was Strasberg's passport to fame, possibly to financial subsidy, and certainly to valuable publicity for The Studio. Strasberg was Marilyn's passport to respectability and to her insistent claims that she wanted to be taken seriously as an actress. As it conflicted with their image of her as a dumb blonde, the media were dubious and patronizing, and when, during an interview, she expatiated for 12 minutes on Stanislavsky, her press agent was accused of writing the material for her. 'Are you kidding?' he replied, '*I* don't know that much about Stanislavsky.' He might have added that the very idea of Marilyn learning a 12 minute speech would have shaken Hollywood to its foundations.

During her time at The Studio, Marilyn participated in two sessions which have since become part of Method mythology. In one, she played the part of Blanche DuBois opposite Lee Strasberg's son, John, in the scene from Tennessee Williams's *A Streetcar Named Desire* where Blanche almost seduces a young delivery boy. In the other, she played the title character in the opening scene of Eugene O'Neill's *Anna Christie*, opposite Maureen Stapleton. Her performances drew applause from those present – an almost unprecedented tribute at Studio sessions. 'I have worked with hundreds and hundreds of actors and actresses,' Strasberg was to tell Joshua Logan in 1956, 'and there are two that stand out way above the rest. Number one is Marlon Brando, and the second is Marilyn Monroe.' On a later occasion he would recall the beauty of those performances and comment that 'when I've often said I saw her as Lady Macbeth, I was not just talking through my hat.' Another observer, the actress Kim Stanley (who had recently triumphed on Broadway in the part of Cherie in *Bus Stop*, which was to be Marilyn's next film role), was to draw on what she had seen for her performance in the Monroe-inspired movie, *The Goddess* (1958).

There has been much critical controversy over whether the Method benefited or damaged Marilyn. Orson Welles's advice to any aspiring actress was: 'They might not like your chemistry; so make sure they admire your technique.' But the Method was never really a discipline for Marilyn: more a form of psychotherapy. It is no coincidence that at about this time, Marilyn began analysis sessions with psychiatrist Marianne Kris. Years later, John Huston, who was astonished by the transformation of talent that had occurred in Marilyn in the decade separating *The Asphalt Jungle* (1950) from *The Misfits* (1961), was to say of Marilyn's approach to acting: 'She went right down into her own personal experience for everything, reached down and pulled something out of herself that was unique and extraordinary. She had no techniques. It was all the truth, it was only Marilyn. But it was Marilyn, plus. She found things about womankind in herself.'

However, others have suggested that psychoanalysis and the Method were the last things Marilyn needed, to help her as an actress or as an individual. Given Billy Wilder's consistently irreverent attitude to psychoanalysis in his movies, it is not surprising that he had some waspish comments on the topic. 'There are certain wonderful rascals in this world, like Monroe,' he said, 'and one day they lie down on an analyst's couch and out comes a clenched, dreary thing. It is better for Monroe not to be straightened out. The charm of her is her

ABOVE: Marilyn seated with Mel Torme at Sunset Strip, with Sammy Davis Jr and Milton Greene behind them. The occasion is Davis's first public appearance since losing an eye in a traffic accident.

LEFT: With Don Murray in *Bus Stop* (1956).

LEFT: Marilyn in 1953 at her most voluptuous.

RIGHT: Enjoying herself on location with *Bus Stop* (1956).

BELOW: With columnist Walter Winchell at a party in 1953.

two left feet. Otherwise she may become a slightly inferior Eva Marie Saint.' On a professional note, there is no doubt that one of the reasons for her terrible working relationship with Sir Laurence Olivier was Olivier's detestation of the Method and Marilyn's devotion to it. On a more personal level, some were afraid that the kind of intense self-analysis demanded by the Method would expose Marilyn to agonizing memories which she could not control, let alone use creatively. 'Beware of staring too long into the abyss,' said the philosopher Nietzsche, 'lest the abyss stare back into thee.' Surely, some of her friends argued, the priority for Marilyn was to shut out her past not face up to it.

BELOW: Partners: Marilyn dances with Arthur Miller.

Nevertheless, if critics and commentators had been condescending about Marilyn's professed acting aspirations during her 14-month sabbatical away from Hollywood, they were soon forced to eat their words. In *Bus Stop* (1956), adapted by George Axelrod from William Inge's Broadway success, Marilyn played the role of a 'chantoose' Cherie at a Phoenix night-club whose dreams of stardom in Hollywood are rudely interrupted by a Montana cowboy (Don Murray) who proposes marriage. The material basically pits her fragile illusions against his relentlessly raucous reality. As it was a role with which Marilyn could easily identify, it provided an invaluable continuity from her classes at The Actors' Studio. It is one of her rare movies in which there is an immediate sense that she feels completely at home.

Helping to coax the best out of Marilyn was director Joshua Logan, a man of the theater who, unlike Lee Strasberg, had actually studied under Stanislavsky. This immediately earned him Marilyn's respect, the absolute minimum requirement needed for a director to have any kind of working relationship with her. Logan was not the best filmmaker Marilyn was to work for – even his better movies, such as *Picnic* (1956) and *Camelot* (1967) never transcend their stage origins - but he was probably the most sympathetic and supportive. He has since described Marilyn as 'the most constantly exciting actress I had ever worked with' and was full of praise for what he called the 'Chaplinesque quality of pathos' she brought to the role. One of the highlights of the film is her rendition of 'That Old Black Magic' as part of Cherie's night-club routine. Logan suggested they film the number as an entity rather than a bit at a time, which was Marilyn's usual procedure. As he calculated, Marilyn's own nervousness and hesitancy about this (quite apart from the song, there is a complicated bit of business where she has to find a kick-switch to change the color of the lighting to a garish red) fuse with those of the character she is playing, and in effect she becomes Cherie. It is one of the most effective cameos of characterization in her career.

Perhaps because of her tutelage by Strasberg and the prestige of her partnership with Milton Greene, people noticed a new assertiveness in Marilyn. For the first time, she took an active part in choosing costumes for the role and was very firm about what she wanted. Inevitably the production had its flashpoints of tension, as did all Marilyn's major films. She and Logan sometimes clashed over the degree of realism required. She was, for example, incensed when he cut a shot of saliva dripping from her lips after a love scene with Don Murray. Jealous of the attention Logan was giving to her co-star, Marilyn in one scene flicked the 'tail' of her costume in Murray's face with unnecessary force, slashing his cheek and causing the actor to stride off the set in a fury. Similar insecurity reared its head when Marilyn had to be assured that the color of a supporting actress's hair was not so blonde that it might distract attention from Marilyn's. Ominously, since it was a recurring threat in the future, illness affected the shooting schedule when Marilyn had to be hospitalized for a fortnight with a bronchial infection.

However, when the film was released, it was a great commercial and critical success, with particular praise for Marilyn's performance. 'Hold on to your chairs, everybody, and get set for a rattling surprise,' wrote the influential Bosley Crowther in *The New York Times*, 'Marilyn Monroe has finally proved herself an actress in *Bus Stop*.' The tone was excessively patronizing but at least the enthusiasm seemed genuine. Since then critics have looked for touches in her performance that might be traceable to her Method training: the tiny embarrassed pause she inserts before the phrase 'that loving stuff'; the way her growing love for Murray is conveyed by the manner in which she touches his jacket. Many regard this not only as her finest performance but of Academy Award standard. It was to be a grave disappointment to her that she was not even nominated. Her performance has stood the test of time as well as, if not better than, any of the actual nominees, who for the record were Carroll Baker in *Baby Doll*, Katharine Hepburn in *The Rainmaker*, Nancy Kelly in *The Bad Seed*, Deborah Kerr in *The King and I*, and – the eventual winner – Ingrid Bergman in *Anastasia*.

Bus Stop was not the only event of 1956 to force the media to drastically re-evaluate their conception of Marilyn. The other was her marriage to the playwright Arthur Miller. In their first meetings several years before, they had discovered an immediate rapport and had begun corresponding. In one early letter, Miller encouraged Marilyn to 'bewitch' the public with 'this image that they ask for,' but he went on: 'I hope and almost pray you won't be hurt in this game or ever change.' When Marilyn left Hollywood for New York in 1954 after the break-up of her marriage to DiMaggio, it is likely that Miller, as well as the Method, was the magnet. The romance began in earnest after Miller divorced his first wife and Marilyn had obtained her divorce. They were married on 29 June 1956.

It seemed like one of the unlikeliest showbiz marriages of all time. It was portrayed as such by the media, who were quite fascinated by this strange conjunction of mind and body. Why was the cinema's leading sex symbol getting married to the bespectacled intellectual playwright of such heavyweight American classics as *All My Sons* (written, 1947; filmed, 1948), *Death of a Salesman* (written, 1949; filmed, 1952) and *The Crucible* (written, 1952; filmed, 1956)? The answer was simple: love at first sight. Miller was dazzled by Marilyn's beauty, charmed by her wit and gaiety, touched by her desire to better herself, and haunted by a quality he sensed of inner sadness. For Marilyn, Miller was one of those lover/

BELOW: Marilyn and her new husband, playwright Arthur Miller.

father/teacher figures whom she could adore for his wisdom and experience.

Miller's relationship with Marilyn had a complex impact on his writing. At first it seemed completely to inhibit him. Later, as a sort of exorcism, it was to become one of his central preoccupations, as a screenwriter, as dramatist, and most recently as autobiographer. The most explicit of his plays about their relationship was to be *After the Fall* (1964), written after her death and about their torments. As shall be seen, his screenplay for *The Misfits* (1961) pays homage to the woman he loved.

Curiously, one of his most important plays of this time, *A View From the Bridge* (written, 1955; filmed, 1962), might also have subconsciously been about him and Marilyn. Although the play is mainly concerned with the self-betrayal of an informer – a key issue of McCarthyist America – it was also about the love of an older man for a younger woman, a love so overpowering that he sensed it could destroy him. 'Marilyn was a whirling light to me then,' Miller was to recall, 'all paradox and enticing mystery, street tough one moment, then lifted by a lyrical and poetic sensitivity.' But even amidst this radiance there was a perplexing darkness that he barely understood. She was, he said, the saddest girl he had ever met.

What bound them together most powerfully at this stage was a sense of mutual respect – for Marilyn, in particular, a commodity most rare. Miller appreciated Marilyn's intelligence and passionately resented the tone of superciliousness, superiority and suggestiveness adopted by the press whom he described as 'slavering imbeciles.' For her part, Marilyn revered his writing but even more his ideas. 'He introduced me to the importance of political freedom in our society,' she said. She could not have chosen a more provocative time to say it.

During the period when they were making preparations for their wedding, Miller was having his much-publicized run-in with the House of UnAmerican Activities Committee, who were investigating alleged Communist infiltration of the entertainment industry and insisting that witnesses demonstrate their patriotism by

FAR RIGHT: American royalty: arriving with Arthur Miller at a Royal Film Performance in London.

BELOW: With Miller, Simone Signoret and Yves Montand.

naming people whom they believed had been Communist Party members. Miller had written *The Crucible* in 1952 as an indictment of the hysteria and witch-hunt mentality of the time. When a friend Elia Kazan had named names and made *On the Waterfront* (1954) which, in Miller's eyes, glorified the informer, Miller had written *A View From the Bridge* (1955) as a riposte and broken with Kazan (they were later to be reconciled).

Miller steadfastly refused to name names. 'I am not protecting the Communists or the Communist Party,' he said, 'I am trying to, and I will, protect my sense of myself. I could not use the name of another person and bring trouble on him.' Yet it is debatable whether the Committee was as impressed by his argument as by his association with Marilyn. Her support for him was total and, no doubt sensing they risked unpopularity if they persecuted the husband of the most popular woman in America, the Committee backed off. Indeed, Miller had been promised a lenient time if he would allow an important Committee member to be photographed with Marilyn, but Miller had refused. After some wrangling, Miller's confiscated passport was returned to him, which enabled him to accompany Marilyn to England for the making of her next film, *The Prince and the Showgirl* (1957), with Laurence Olivier.

The film was based on a play by Terence Rattigan, *The Sleeping Prince*, which is about the romance between an arrogant Ruritanian prince and a chorus-girl, who meet when in London for the coronation of George V in 1911. The play had been a modest success on Broadway, and Marilyn had bought the screen rights in the first move of her business partnership with Milton Greene. When it was announced that she was to co-star with Laurence Olivier, everyone seemed enchanted by the prospect. 'The most exciting combination since black and white, ' said Joshua Logan who, when asked by Olivier, gave him some advice about how to handle Marilyn. 'Don't lose your temper with her,' he said, 'or you'll lose her.' He added – prophetically, as it turned out – that whatever difficulties he encountered in extracting a performance from Marilyn, he would be amazed by the result. Whether that compensated sufficiently for the difficulties is debatable. Marilyn felt a twinge of foreboding when she learned that Olivier was planning to direct as well as act in the film, but felt that she was too committed to the production at that stage to back out. Olivier himself was to regret taking on the additional burden of direction as problem after problem began to

mount with the production of the film.

Yet when Olivier first met her to discuss the project, he had been bowled over and, as he candidly confessed, ready to fall in love. She had kept him and the assembled guests waiting, of course, until he had shouted, 'Come on, Marilyn, for God's sake, you know we're all dying to see you.' At which point she appeared and, according to Olivier, had everyone at her feet within seconds. What then went wrong?

Initially there were small niggles that eventually assumed massive proportions. Olivier was annoyed when she arrived an hour late for her first London press conference, for he had spent considerable energy in exhorting her to be on time and thus confound the image the media had of her as the scatter-brained sex-queen. Her lateness seemed like calculated disobedience, even though it was not. Then, prior to the start of shooting, Olivier insisted on a rehearsal period so that the cast could get to know one another. It was not intended as a tactless gesture but it threw Marilyn, who was used to constructing her performances from tiny units of instinct and intensity, into a blind panic.

ABOVE: In England for the making of *The Prince and the Showgirl* (1957), Marilyn and her husband, Arthur Miller, are greeted by Olivier and his wife, Vivien Leigh (who had played Marilyn's role on stage).

FAR LEFT: Marilyn with Lawrence Olivier at a press conference at the Savoy Hotel, London for *The Prince and the Showgirl*.

ABOVE: Marilyn and her dark angel: her black-clad drama coach, Paula Strasberg.

FAR RIGHT: Two striking views of Marilyn in *The Prince and the Showgirl* (1957).

Thereafter things went from bad to worse. Marilyn was frequently late and, according to Olivier, 'grew ruder and more insolent.' Some observers said that her demeanor was that of a naughty child daring her teacher to spank her. Olivier in turn was progressively irritated by the constant, somber presence of the black-clad Paula Strasberg, ostensibly Marilyn's dramatic coach but whom Olivier thought had only one talent: 'to butter Marilyn up.' According to Michael Korda's account of a conversation he had with Milton Greene, relations deteriorated to the point where Olivier was telling Marilyn to her face that she had body odor and ought to wash more.

Undoubtedly, the main difficulty, though, was the conflict between their attitudes to acting. Marilyn was under the influence of the Method and Strasberg's inspirational teaching, and could not relate in any way to what she saw as Olivier's mechanical approach to direction. Olivier was hostile to the Method and felt its all-consuming passion for reality, psychological truth and personal relevance blithely ignored basic technique and training. One day he walked on to the set and simply instructed Marilyn to 'be sexy,' at which point she promptly walked off and put in a long-distance phone call to Lee Strasberg. How could you simply 'be sexy' if you had not first attuned yourself to the images and memories that would

make 'sexiness' seem personally real and authentic? Some found Marilyn's reaction excessive: Strasberg thought Olivier's direction insensitive. The last straw for Olivier was the time when he had tried every trick he could think of in terms of direction to make Marilyn scintillate more in a scene but nothing seemed to work until Paula Strasberg spoke up: 'Honey, just think of Coca-Cola and Frank Sinatra.' At that point, said Olivier, he was ready to give up.

The tension between the two stars put a strain on Marilyn's marriage. Arthur Miller was forced into acting the rather demeaning role of mediator between the two. Given the nature of the conflict between the stars, it did not help that Miller shared some of Olivier's reservations about Strasberg as an acting teacher, although he interpreted Marilyn's idealization of Strasberg as a generous impulse of faith after years in the Hollywood jungle. Also Miller was temperamentally rather similar to Olivier, solid and rational. The two also possibly saw similarities in their situation of both being married to highly volatile actress-wives, Olivier at this time still being married to Vivien Leigh. Even with the best of intentions, Miller must have found it hard to provide the unqualified support that Marilyn demanded, and needed.

There is the story too that Marilyn found a wounding reference to herself in Miller's personal journal that compared her to his first wife. An incident like this was to be dramatized in Miller's autobiographical play, *After the Fall* (1964), so it is quite likely to have happened. In her state of unhappiness, Marilyn could only have interpreted such a reference as an act of betrayal. It all added to the tense atmosphere.

Such suffering seems out of all proportion to the trifle on which they were all engaged. Somehow they all got through it, and Marilyn even had the grace to apologize to the crew for any difficulty she had caused. On one occasion when Marilyn had been late again through illness, Dame Sybil Thorndike remarked: 'We need her desperately. She's the only one of us who knows how to act in front of the camera.' And when he viewed the final film away from the traumas of shooting, Olivier had to marvel at the contrast between the apparent limpness of Marilyn on the set and the impact of her on the screen. On the set, the only scene which had created no difficulty was the coronation sequence, where she had no dialogue and took direction, in Olivier's phrase, 'like a lamb.' On the screen, she glowed throughout. 'Marilyn was quite wonderful, the best of all,' Olivier generously admitted, adding: 'So. What do you know?'

The experience of working on *The Prince and the Showgirl* had taken a heavy toll on all of the major participants, and was to continue to do so even after the close of shooting. It had been thanks to Milton Greene's skillful management that, for all the difficulties, the film had still been completed under budget, yet Greene's days as Marilyn's business partner were numbered. The main conflict here was not with Marilyn but with Arthur Miller. Inevitably, as husband and as an unofficial but very prestigious artistic adviser, Miller began taking an interest in Marilyn's affairs that impinged on Greene's territory. Miller would criticize aspects of Marilyn's publicity; he began to advise on scripts. Greene was gradually made to feel redundant and eventually, with a fee of $100,000, he was paid off.

For the next year, Marilyn took a rest from the cinema, and she and Arthur Miller divided their time mainly between their apartment in Manhattan and their new home in the country in the Roxbury area of Connecticut. Miller was working on a new story, which was eventually to become his screenplay for *The Misfits* (1961), and much of it was to be inspired by things he noticed about Marilyn in this natural setting, particularly her hypersensitivity to cruelty to animals.

During this time, just when Marilyn seemed to be recovering her strength, some

ABOVE: What a pussycat: Marilyn with friend.

LEFT: An earnest Marilyn tells reporters about her acting ambitions at the Plaza Hotel, New York, in February 1956.

ABOVE: Autograph hunters at the airport for Marilyn's thirtieth birthday.

RIGHT: Ready to depart for a holiday in Jamaica.

blow would knock her sideways. She suffered a miscarriage in 1957, and her dependence on sleeping pills almost resulted on one occasion in a fatal barbiturate coma. A fragment of a poem she wrote in 1958 ('Help I feel life coming closer/When all I want to do is to die') gives a feel of her depressive state, which was not constant but intermittently overwhelming. Only two things seemed likely to snap her out of it: a long-desired baby; or a great film. By the time she started work on her next film in 1958, Billy Wilder's successful *Some Like It Hot*, she was pregnant.

In *Some Like It Hot* (1959), Marilyn plays a singer, Sugar Kane, in an all-girls band called Sweet Sue's Society Syncopaters. She becomes involved with two new musicians in the band, who are actually two men (Tony Curtis and Jack Lemmon) disguised as girls because they have inadvertently witnessed a gangland massacre and are being pursued by Spats Columbo (George Raft) and his hoodlums. Marilyn's character is an alcoholic romantic and sexual victim, not very bright, unlucky in love, and always winding up with the 'fuzzy end of the lollipop' and the 'squeezed-out tube of toothpaste.'

At the outset, apparently, Marilyn and Miller had some misgivings about the script. It offered her another of her dumb

BELOW: Marilyn relaxes, as photographed by Milton Greene in 1956.

showgirl roles and moreover reduced her to a mere comic foil to her male co-stars. Marilyn also felt she could not make the central situation, of a character being attracted to two men in drag, believable. 'But Marilyn,' said Lee Strasberg when she consulted him about this, 'you've always talked about your difficulty in having friendships with other women because they instinctively regard you as a rival and as a threat. Now here suddenly are two women and they want to be your friend. They like you. For the first time in your life, you have two girlfriends.' Marilyn saw that she could relate to that and, for the moment, the central situation fell into place for her. During the shooting, very little else did.

The anguish behind the making of *Some Like It Hot* has become almost as famous as the movie itself, perhaps because of the sheer dichotomy between the agony (of the making) and the ecstasy (of the finished product). Unlike Olivier, Billy Wilder was not bothered by the presence of Paula Strasberg on the set: on the contrary, it reassured him that at least someone could still communicate with Marilyn, since he was finding it increasingly difficult. 'We were in midflight,' he was to say later, 'and there was a nut on the plane.'

First, there was Marilyn's compulsive lateness, which now sometimes stretched to six hours, escalating costs and leaving her co-stars hanging around in heavy and

ABOVE: Sweet Sue's Society Syncopaters in *Some Like It Hot* (1959): Tony Curtis on tenor sax, Jack Lemmon on double bass, and Marilyn on ukelele.

BELOW: Marilyn admires Jack Lemmon's figure as they frolic on Miami beach in *Some Like It Hot* (1959).

FAR RIGHT: Marilyn's sultry performance as Sugar Kane in *Some Like It Hot* was to earn her many accolades.

uncomfortable make-up under hot arc lamps. During the shooting, Arthur Miller asked if, in consideration of her pregnancy, Marilyn could be let off at 4.30pm. 'But Arthur,' replied Wilder, 'she's only ever ready to start at 4 – what does she do all morning?' At times Wilder was philosophical about the problem. 'I have an Aunt Ida in Vienna who is always on time,' he would say, 'but then I wouldn't put her in a movie – do you get my point?' Less philosophical was Tony Curtis, who had most of the long scenes with Marilyn and who could not emulate Wilder's external calm. When asked by a reporter how he had enjoyed kissing Marilyn, Curtis made his now famous remark: 'It was like kissing Hitler.' Marilyn said he was only jealous because she got to wear prettier dresses than he did.

Then there was her chronic inability to remember lines. This reached its highest art in *Some Like It Hot* in a scene where a distraught Sugar has to burst into the hotel room of her drag friends in search of alcoholic solace. Marilyn's line, 'Where's the bourbon?' required 59 takes.

What was most disconcerting, however, was her unpredictability. On some days she was fine, which threw everyone. Also her comments on her role were often astute. She sensed that the entrance of her character was not strong enough and mentioned this to Wilder. On reflection, he agreed and, with co-writer I A L Diamond, came up with something better – the famous moment when Sugar walks along the platform and the train lets out a jet of steam as she passes, almost like a wolf whistle. The sexual vibrations given off by Sugar are such that even a machine responds.

To Wilder's amazement, her long scene on the beach with Curtis, who is now disguised as a Miami millionaire, was done in two takes. It is the finest piece of sustained comedy acting she accomplished on screen, with every nuance of the brilliant dialogue shaded, captured and perfectly timed. When Curtis explains that he is clutching his basket of shells to remind him of the company he owns, Marilyn exclaims 'Shell Oil!' her face dropping and her eyes rolling as disbelief and desire come into mad collision. It is one of the funniest reaction shots one could ever hope to see in screen comedy. 'There were stretches,' Wilder has said, 'when she was absolutely phenomenal: one of the great comediennes.' The beach scene was one of those stretches.

What was Marilyn's problem during the making of *Some Like It Hot?* It was partly the difficulty in reconciling Strasbergian techniques to high comedy. The Method might help an actor come to terms with the psychodramas of Tennessee Williams or William Inge, but it is not so readily applicable to nine out of ten of American plays, or

screenplays. But mainly the problem was one of illness, and an increasing dependence on a lethal combination of drink and drugs, often encasing her in a mental fog. The production ended unhappily. A day after the completion of shooting, Marilyn was rushed into hospital and had another miscarriage. Having kept himself under control during the agonizing five months of shooting, Wilder let slip in an interview some intemperate remarks about working with Monroe ('I am now sleeping at night and can sit across the table from my wife and not feel like hitting her because she is a woman.') It prompted an angry exchange of telegrams between Billy Wilder and Arthur Miller.

Seen 30 years on, and away from all this backstage rancor, *Some Like It Hot* still retains its place as one of the greatest of all Hollywood comedies, and Marilyn is indispensable to its magic. She has less of the laughter than Jack Lemmon, and Wilder's naughtiest trick is to ensure that her most passionate screen kiss is delivered to her by Tony Curtis in drag. Yet no film has been more sensitive to her sweetness, her bruised romanticism, her awesomely appealing combination of Earth Mother and frightened child. Her midnight feast with Daphne (Jack Lemmon) on the upper berth of the train definitively enshrines her movie innocence. Her rendering of the song, 'I'm Through With Love,' as no other moment in her films, plumbs the depths of sadness behind her fabulous, fun-loving façade. Even as *Some Like It Hot* was being acclaimed as her movie monument, her sadness was opening up before her like an abyss.

ABOVE: Monroe by Beaton.

Chapter Five

SOMETHING'S GOT TO GIVE

The Final Years (1960-1962)

'She was "Marilyn Monroe" and that was what was killing her. And it could not be otherwise for her; she lived on film and with that glory forsworn would in some real sense vanish.' ARTHUR MILLER

Marilyn's next movie, *Let's Make Love* (1960), could hardly have looked a more routine vehicle: basically, the billionaire and the showgirl. The only twist was that the billionaire would be required to pretend to be an accomplished comedian and song-and-dance man, in order to be near the showgirl and also to ensure that she falls in love with him and not his money.

The film's credentials seemed strong enough. The writer was the brilliant scenarist, Norman Krasna, whose speciality lay in the comic permutations of mistaken identity, and the director was the redoubtable George Cukor, acknowledged master of the backstage comedy-drama. Yet with everyone performing below par and even with guest appearances from Bing Crosby and Gene Kelly failing to enliven things, *Let's Make Love* became less notable for its gaiety on screen than for the gossip it engendered offscreen, notably the hot news item that its stars, Marilyn Monroe and Yves Montand, seemed to be taking the title literally.

The casting of Yves Montand in the role of the billionaire was a peculiar stroke of fate. For one thing, he was completely miscast. The whole basis of the comedy, Norman Krasna explained, was Dr Johnson's observation on a dog walking on its hind legs: 'it is not done well but you are surprised to find it done at all.' In other words, the humor was not in the disguise itself, but in the incongruity of a man such as that attempting that kind of disguise. The film needed an actor whom an audience would instantly recognize as someone who cannot sing, dance, or tell jokes — a Gary Cooper, Krasna thought, or a Gregory Peck. So the film casts a man who is not only unknown to the majority of the audience but is one of the world's most compelling song performers. Small wonder the joke fell flat.

The other irony was that Montand had apparently been suggested for the role by Arthur Miller, an admirer of Montand and his wife, Simone Signoret, since they had acted the main roles in a French stage production of *The Crucible* (roles they would later repeat on film). Also their radical political views were in harmony with the Millers, so the two married couples became good friends. It was during a period while Miller was away in New York and Signoret was filming in France that an affair started between Montand and Monroe. It became public knowledge when the queen-bee of the gossip columnists, Hedda Hopper, ran an interview with Montand in which she quoted him as saying that Marilyn had a 'schoolgirl crush' on him.

Discussing the episode in her autobiography, *Nostalgia Isn't What It Used To Be*, Simone Signoret displayed the same calmness she had exhibited at the time. She queried whether Montand had actually said that to Miss Hopper — as Signoret pointed out, his English was just not up to it — and expressed regret that Marilyn 'never knew to what degree I never detested her . . .' In his autobiography Arthur Miller does not mention his wife's affair with Montand at all. As it was worldwide news, he could hardly have been unaware of it. Might he have felt that an affair with so desirable a partner would boost Marilyn's dwindling self-confidence, and that the role of jealous husband would help both of them less than that of silent but understanding friend?

FAR LEFT: Marilyn on the set of *Let's Make Love* (1960).

LEFT and ABOVE:
Marilyn, Miller and
Montand deep in
discussion.

RIGHT: Paula Strasberg
offers friendly advice.

ABOVE: Marilyn chatting with the cameraman of *Let's Make Love* (1960), Dan Fapp.

FAR RIGHT: With Frankie Vaughan in *Let's Make Love*; and, as caught by Inge Morath on the set of *The Misfits* (1961).

Curious if so, and miscalculated, for Marilyn was deeply hurt by Montand's public disclosures. Had Miller consciously closed his eyes to it, steeling himself for the crisis to come? He must have felt that his marriage was in ruins and thought his only course was to get out from under the wreckage as well as he could. By the time *The Misfits* (1961) came round, a script by Miller that

had been designed as a 'gift' to his wife, the text had acquired a mantle of tragic irony.

On the face of it, the project could hardly have appeared more congenial. She was co-starring at last with her all-time screen-hero, Clark Gable. She was working again with the director who had given her her first big break, John Huston. She was sur-rounded by friends in co-starring roles – Eli

Wallach, Kevin McCarthy, Thelma Ritter (with whom she had appeared in *All About Eve* [1950]) and Montgomery Clift (who she had described after their first meeting as 'the only person I know who's in worse shape than I am').

Moreover the script was not only the sort of serious dramatic work she had been craving but had been written expressly for her

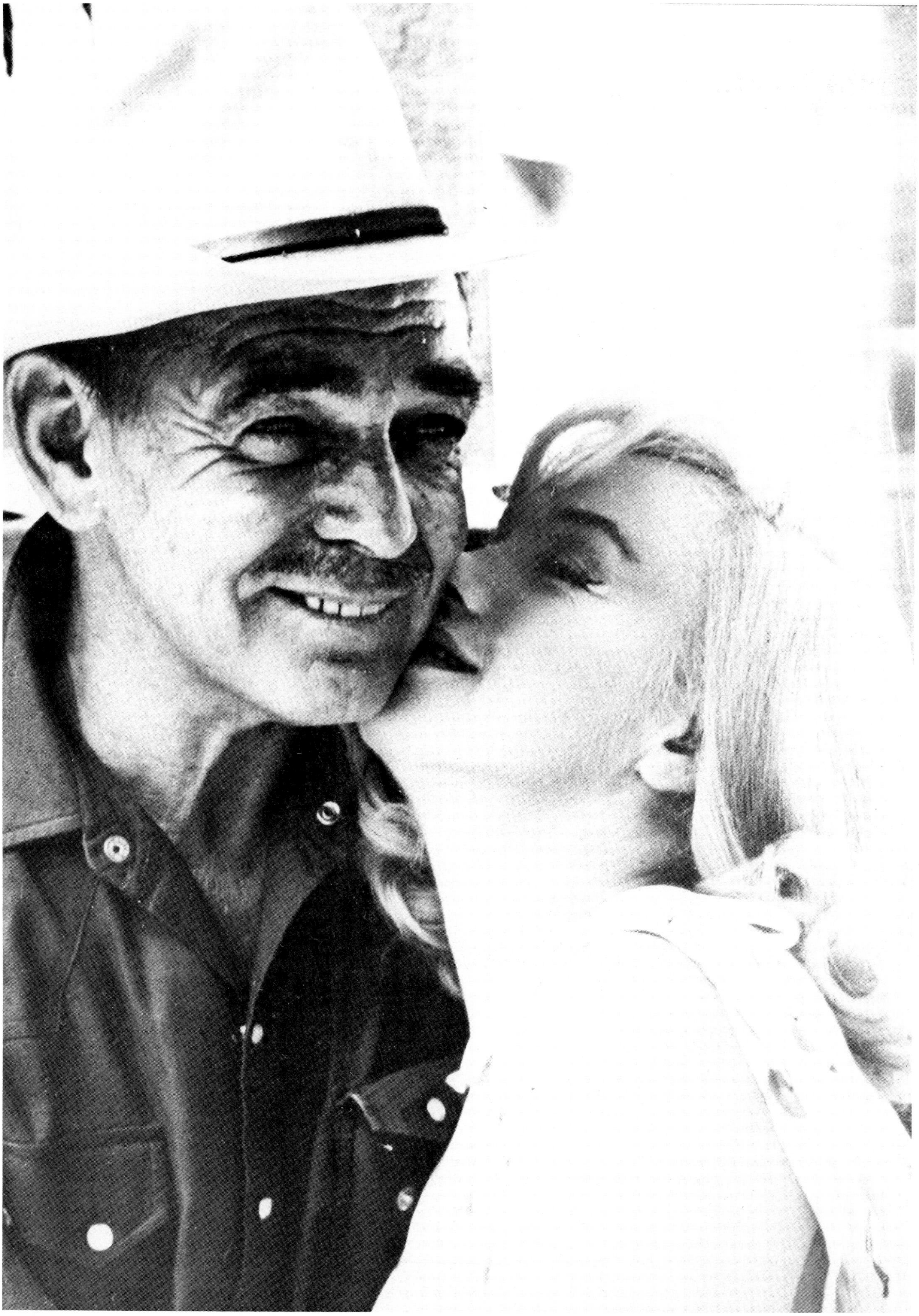

by a great writer who knew her intimately and could catch her spirit with sympathy and poetry. She did not have to act: she only had to be. Marilyn was the heroine Roslyn, the divorcee in Reno who becomes involved with three misfit cowboys, Gay (Gable), Guido (Wallach) and Perce (Clift). For once she seemed to be cast opposite a trio of ideal male co-stars, playing roles that were close to their actual relationship with her – a romantic father-figure (Gable), a devoted friend (Wallach), and a spiritual soul-mate (Clift).

Yet *The Misfits* turned out to be a night-mare in the making and became notorious as one of the most ill-starred, death-haunted movies in Hollywood history. By the time the movie started shooting, Marilyn's marriage to Miller was dying, which gave an added piquancy to the opening scenes where Roslyn is going through with her divorce. As Miller had to be on call almost every day to deal with last-minute revisions and rewrites, the disintegration of his relationship with Monroe took place in full view of the rest of the crew. This in turn led to a situation in which some sided with Marilyn and others with Miller, which hardly contributed to a happy set.

Huston tried to remain aloof and get on

ABOVE: Appearing at last with her screen idol, Clark Gable.

LEFT: Gable as cowboy and Marilyn as divorcee fall in love in *The Misfits* (1961).

ABOVE: *The Misfits* team: producer Frank Taylor (under the ladder), writer Arthur Miller (on top of the ladder), actor Eli Wallach and director John Huston (below). On bottom, left to right: Montgomery Clift, Marilyn Monroe, Clark Gable.

with the film but this proved extremely difficult. On occasions he was appalled at Marilyn's cruelty, particularly on one day when she drove back to her trailer and deliberately left Miller stranded on the desert location: he would have been there all night if Huston had not spotted him. On other occasions he was exasperated by Miller's apparent resignation and lack of resolution, particularly regarding Marilyn's health, though he later conceded that he did not fully understand that the situation had long since got out of Miller's control.

At times Marilyn could be, according to Huston, nothing short of wonderful. But for most of the time she was either late or in such a mental haze that her presence was not much help. Huston was calculating that she was taking up to 20 Nembutal sleeping pills a day, washing them down with a deadly combination of vodka and champagne. Filming had to be halted for two weeks when she was rushed to Westside Hospital in Los Angeles to have her stomach pumped out. Even when she returned, matters did not improve. 'Anyone who allows her to take narcotics ought to be shot,' growled Huston, railing against those Hollywood doctors who were so casually prescribing what Marilyn demanded. With unhappily prophetic accuracy, Huston told Miller that, if Marilyn continued like this, she would either wind up in an asylum or be dead within two or three years.

'What the hell is that girl's problem?' queried Gable in exasperation as he waited day after day for his leading lady to appear. 'Goddamn it, I like her, but she's so damned unprofessional.' Gable was to die of a heart attack less than two weeks after the film had been completed and, tragically, a few months before the birth of his only child. Mingled with Marilyn's grief was a strong sense of guilt, and a suspicion that her shabby treatment of him might have been a form of revenge on the father whom Gable so much resembled. Still, Gable had lived to see a rough cut of the film before his death and thought, rightly, that it was one of the best things he had ever done. It is certainly one of the finest things Marilyn ever did, but it forced Arthur Miller to wonder whether

such torture was really worth it.

In Roslyn, Miller attempted to enshrine permanently on celluloid the Marilyn he loved. He caught all her vulnerability, innocence and idealism, her pain at the impermanence of relationships, and her frequent flinching from the insensitive brutality of the world of men. She has never been paid more glowing compliments on film – 'You shine in my eyes,' 'I bless you, girl,' 'You have the gift for life, Roslyn . . .' Love positively flowed from Miller's pen but in the midst of such eloquence the look of baffled hurt never leaves Marilyn's eyes. Her pain is so acute and visible that, uniquely on film, it is sometimes unbearable to look at her. It is a nakedly emotional performance, the soul of a woman laid bare.

In Gay's conversations with Roslyn, Miller seemed to be recalling things that he himself had told Marilyn – 'What makes you so sad? I think you're the saddest girl I ever

BELOW: Marilyn and Miller chat with John Huston (left). 'Don't think, just do it,' said Huston to Marilyn when she asked him what she should think about when shooting craps. 'That's the story of your life.'

met.' At other times, as in the scene when Roslyn grows hysterical when Gay is preparing to shoot a rabbit, he draws directly on his experience with Marilyn when they lived together in the country. This sensitivity to animals builds up towards the film's main set-piece: a mustang round-up, which becomes a soul-searing shattering of illusions for all the major characters and rouses Roslyn to a paroxysm of anguish and anger.

Roslyn's outburst against the three men is not quite the climax of the film but it is its most heart-rending moment. Sickened now to the point of dementia by the cruelty she has witnessed, she runs out into the white desert and then turns and shrieks at them – 'Butchers! You! Murderers! You liars! You're only happy when you see something die!' That stammering, *staccato* rhythm is all Marilyn's. It is not written like that in the published script and is an incredibly effective way of suggesting the inner torment of a distraught woman now at the end of her

tether. It is hard to pin down precisely the tingling impact of this moment. It is partly to do with Huston's visual framing of it, the words crackling like sheets of lightning out of a bleached and impassive landscape. It owes much to Marilyn's extraordinary vocal performance, for once on screen really letting go, and practically the only time one can remember her shouting at any stage of her film career. Most of all perhaps, the force of the moment is attributable to the fearful fusion at this point between actress and role, so that the speech becomes a doubly disillusioned tirade at the overwhelming bestiality of life. Coincidentally, the day on which they shot this scene happened to be the one occasion on which Lee Strasberg showed up to see what was going on. What must he have thought? Was he awed by the dramatic power he had been instrumental in unleashing in Marilyn? Or was he alarmed by the sound of a psyche shredding itself to pieces?

ABOVE: Montgomery Clift arrives with Marilyn at the Loew's Capitol Theater for a preview screening of *The Misfits* (1961).

ABOVE LEFT: After two weeks in hospital, Marilyn, accompanied by Arthur Miller, returns to complete filming *The Misfits*.

FAR LEFT: A happier moment during the filming of *The Misfits*.

LEFT: With Mexican lover, Jose Bolanos in 1962.

RIGHT: At The Actors' Studio after her illness in 1961, and even beginning to look like Paula Strasberg.

With hindsight one can see that *The Misfits* marked the beginning of the end. By now Marilyn was seriously ill. On the advice of her psychiatrist, she was admitted to the Payne Whitney Psychiatric Clinic in New York for a period of rest and consultation. There cannot have been a more terrifying environment for someone with a repressed apprehension that the madness in her family history was being revisited in her. After 10 days, she was rescued by Joe DiMaggio who had reappeared on hearing of Marilyn's impending divorce. It is unclear whether his motives were entirely selfless or whether he was hoping for a reconciliation, but for whatever reason, he was to offer stalwart support during her final months.

Was Marilyn's popularity by now on the wane? Sex-goddesses, like sports stars, have a limited time-span at their peak and, irrespective of ability, it is hard to imagine Marilyn managing a smooth transition to character actress. Nevertheless, there were intriguing projects being discussed. Lee Strasberg wanted to do a television production with her of Somerset Maugham's *Rain*. One of Marilyn's most ardent admirers, Jean-Paul Sartre was working on a screenplay about Freud for John Huston, and badly wanted Marilyn to play the main female role. Despite such plans, her physical and mental health were so fragile that neither project looked feasible. She had now acquired a new psychiatrist, Dr Ralph Greenson and thanks to his kindness and solicitude, a new adopted family. He soon discovered that he had taken on a patient who was not only a depressive and insomniac but also a borderline schizophrenic.

The year 1962 was to see reversals and rejections, when one betrayal too many tipped Marilyn over the edge. The major professional blow came with a film she was doing for Fox to see out the end of her contract that now, with inflated star salaries, looked a lot less generous than it had in 1956 when it was drawn up. At $100,000 per picture, they were now getting Marilyn cheap.

LEFT: Rumors of reconciliation: Marilyn strolls on a Florida beach with DiMaggio in March 1961.

FAR LEFT: Marilyn receives a Golden Globe award from Rock Hudson as 'world film favorite' in 1961.

Something's Got To Give was a remake of a Cary Grant/Irene Dunne hit of 1940, *My Favorite Wife*, about a wife, presumed drowned, who returns to find her husband has remarried. The movie was eventually to be made as *Move Over, Darling* (1963), starring Doris Day. Marilyn was not around to see it.

Marilyn had liked Nunnally Johnson's original script but when director George Cukor came in and proposed rewrites, she probably felt her judgment was being called into question and thus became a lot less enthusiastic. When Walter Bernstein met her to discuss the script (he was by then the seventh writer to be engaged on the project), she seemed an odd mixture of modesty and narcissism, hesitancy and intransigence. By the time shooting started, faith in the project had plummeted and Marilyn's confidence and health were at rock-bottom.

In 35 days of shooting, Marilyn managed to attend only 12, during which she walked off the set when she suspected her co-star Dean Martin of having a cold, and became paranoid about the color of Cyd Charisse's hair ('her unconscious thinks it's blonde,' she is alleged to have said). Even though the film was behind schedule, Marilyn took time off to open a charity game at the Dodgers Stadium and also to attend President Kennedy's birthday gala with Arthur Miller's father, at which she sang 'Happy Birthday To You' to a delighted President. Twentieth Century Fox were not delighted.

The studio became even more alarmed when they saw the rushes. Marilyn had done a nude scene in the swimming pool which was stunning – the photographs of the scene were to make almost as big a splash when published as the nude calendar pictures. Elsewhere, though, she seemed lifeless and vacant, like a sleepwalker. In the past, she had been nursed through spells like this, often to spectacular effect, as her final performances in *Some Like It Hot* (1959) and *The Misfits* (1961) testify. But this time was different. While Fox might have been expected to show some sympathy for her distress (she had, after all, made more money for the studio than any other star of the last decade), the company was currently too embroiled in another massive production, *Cleopatra* (1963), whose costs were getting out of control. They took a drastic step, firing Monroe and initiating a lawsuit against her. When Dean Martin promptly resigned from the film in protest, they sued him too.

Some days later, members of the film's crew placed an advertisement in *Variety*, sarcastically 'thanking' Marilyn for the sort

of self-centered star behavior which had put them all out of work. She sent each of them a message pleading it was not her fault. When he saw the advertisement, Arthur Miller, who understood better than anyone Marilyn's feelings of comradeship with these people, recognized that 'nothing could have wounded her more deeply.' Marilyn's troubles seemed to be advancing in battalions. Her sense of persecution was no doubt fanned still further by the concurrent happiness of Miller who since their divorce,

ABOVE: A slimmer Marilyn prepares for her new film, *Something's Got To Give*.

FAR LEFT: Still looking gorgeous: Marilyn during the ill-fated shooting of *Something's Got To Give*.

LEFT and RIGHT: The famous nude shots from *Something's Got To Give*, as photographed by Lawrence Schiller. When published after her death, they created as great a stir as her nude calendar pose 13 years earlier. The body is still beautiful, but the face looks tense rather than innocent.

ABOVE: Marilyn in *Something's Got To Give*. Some of the footage was seen in the compilation film, *Marilyn*, released by Fox a year after her death.

FAR RIGHT: Marilyn's body is being moved from the mortuary, prior to being transported to the morgue in downtown Los Angeles.

had married Inge Morath, a photographer who had covered the filming of *The Misfits* (1961). In what must have seemed to Marilyn at that low time a bitter mockery of her own barrenness, they were now expecting their first child. By contrast, Marilyn was losing weight at a worrying rate.

Then came her association with the Kennedys. It is now a truism that the recurrent tragic flaw in the Kennedy character has been an insatiable appetite for women. Gloria Swanson had been caught up in their amorous intrigues a generation earlier: Marilyn was the new glittering prize. From the most authoritative accounts of this period in her life, particularly Anthony Summers' biography *Goddess* (1985), it seems that Marilyn had a casual affair with President John Kennedy, and also a much deeper involvement with the President's brother, the Attorney General, Robert (Bobby) Kennedy which may have led to pregnancy and abortion.

The effect of all this on an already battered ego can be imagined, not to mention the political fall-out that could have ensued.

Given Marilyn's involvement with the Campaign for a Safe Nuclear Policy, an affair with a President whose relations with his Soviet counterpart Kruschev were at their lowest point, could hardly have been more disastrously timed: it constituted not only a scandal but a security risk. An affair with an Attorney General who was investigating organized crime in America was not simply romantically risky but political dynamite: Marilyn was not simply an extramarital fling but an instrument of potential blackmail. In the last years of her life, the surveillance of Marilyn undoubtedly passed out of the province of the mere press publicist and into that of more senior and expert practitioners – the FBI, the CIA and the Mafia.

Yet, in an interview with the journalist W J Weatherby that year, Marilyn hinted at a possible marriage with a very prominent politician. He had little doubt that she meant Bobby Kennedy and he was worried, not by the remote prospect of such a marriage but by the impact on her of the inevitable let-down. The realization that she had been used, that she was no longer needed, might be unbearable.

The whole truth might never be known about precisely what happened on Marilyn's last night alive. Believing it was the night Bobby Kennedy made clear to her the affair was over and that she was being discarded, George Cukor commented: 'It was a nasty business, her worst rejection. Power and money. In the end she was too innocent.' Lee Strasberg's son, John, made the same judgment of the way powerful people took advantage of her: 'People looked at her like a thing; they thought about what she was worth to them.' Was her death precipitated by Kennedy's goodbye, which in a life of abandonments, was the final and fatal straw? Was the death deliberate or an accident – Marilyn dying in the act of reaching for the phone and calling for help? These, and other, questions have reverberated unsettlingly over the years, but the bare facts were shocking enough: on the Saturday night of 4 August 1962, Marilyn Monroe died, officially from an overdose of barbiturates.

The immediate aftermath of the death was strange, even chilling. Nobody claimed what was once the most desired body in the world. Her make-up man, Whitey Snyder fulfilled a morbid promise he had made to her a decade before and performed his final cosmetic miracle on the corpse while it was still warm: the make-up man as mortician. And the funeral arrangements were made by a man she had divorced nearly ten years ago, Joe DiMaggio. For the 'saddest girl,' it was the loneliest death imaginable.

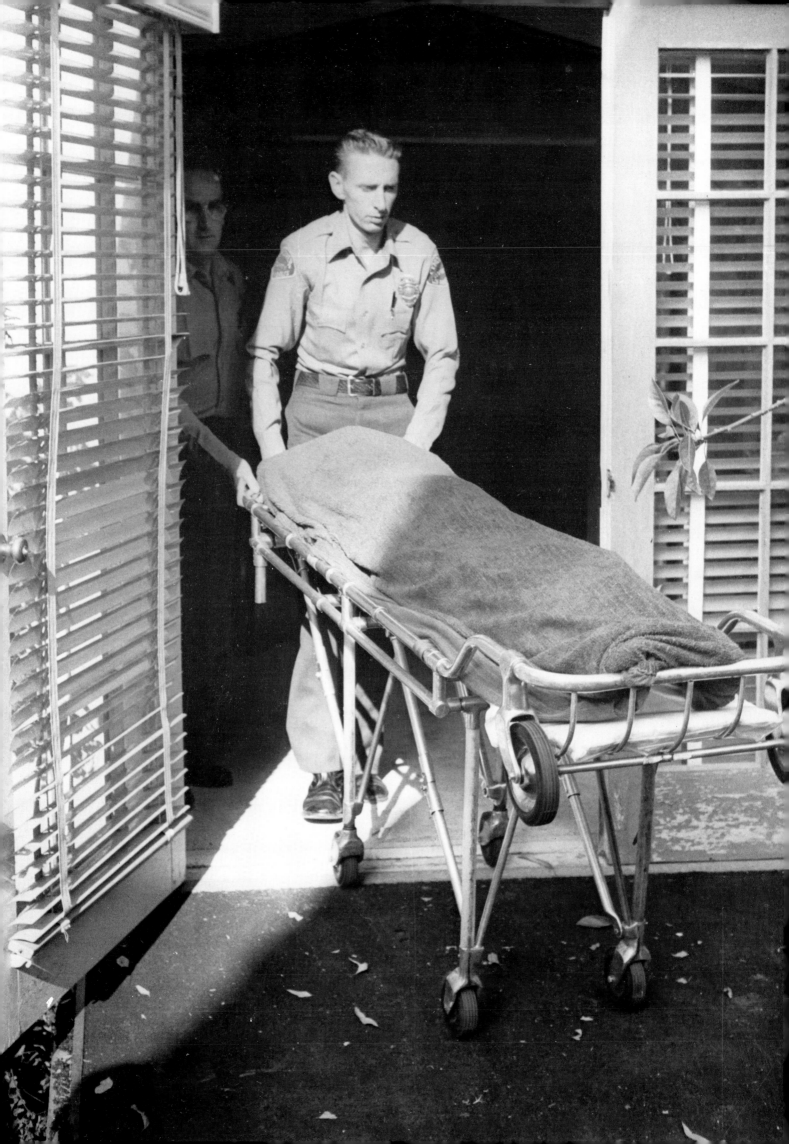

Chapter Six

THE ELUSIVE MARILYN

'She was a poet on a street corner trying to recite to a crowd pulling at her clothes.' ARTHUR MILLER

'I'll tell you what becomes a legend most. Not sticking around beyond your time. Monroe and Harlow – they were the lucky ones.' The Countess in Billy Wilder's *Fedora*

When the news broke of Elvis Presley's sudden death, a journalist was heard to comment: 'Smart career move.' A cynical remark, but with a grain of accuracy. As James Dean also demonstrated, nothing is more conducive to myth than premature death. So it was with Marilyn. It is hard to imagine a Monroe of over 60, which is the age she would be today. If many of the circumstances of her death were appalling, in one sense her death was merciful and how she would have wished it, for at least she died when still beautiful.

Yet there are reasons other than premature death why the Marilyn Monroe story has become the stuff of modern legend. There are the mysteries surrounding her death, which to this day have not been solved and which made it a political as well as showbiz event. Even in her starlet days, because of her association with the radical Actors' Lab and Arthur Miller, Marilyn had been peripherally caught up in the anti-Communist hysteria of the 1950s. Because of her involvement with the Kennedys, she was to become a central symbol during the political paranoia of the 1960s and 1970s. Marilyn's death was the first in a series of violent deaths of outstanding public figures that remain cloaked in enigma. Her fate became a crucial contribution to a modern concept of history as the political art of conspiracy. For one of Marilyn's most thorough biographers, Anthony Summers, this was the key aspect of her story. 'In this era of canned news and dwindling press effort truly to inform,' he said, 'may the Marilyn Monroe story move people to insist, urgently, on their right to know.'

The truth about her death is elusive but no more so than the truth about her life. How much can one believe about someone who felt she had so much to conceal; who, from childhood, had learned the orphan's safety-mechanism of secretiveness; and who, because of the plots of her movies and the smokescreen of her publicity, could be forgiven for blurring the line between fantasy and fact? She may or may not have endured attempted suffocation or sexual seduction, or both, in childhood. In her adult life, she had three broken marriages – or was it four? 'How many children had Lady Macbeth?' used to be a popular investigative sport among literary critics. For the modern biographer, the equivalent question would be: how many abortions had Marilyn Monroe? Small wonder that so many writers keep finding new pieces of this most splintered of stars, wondering where they might fit, puzzling to see if they form a complete picture.

Basic facts about Marilyn are a problem and equally difficult is making sense of what facts there are. How does one reconcile all the facets of this woman, which seem not simply diverse but contradictory? For example, there is the contrast between the image she projected on screen and the impression she made off it. Olivier was surprised by her wit, and an amazed Clifford Odets commented to Arthur Miller, 'She reads, doesn't she?' as if he had discovered exceptional precociousness in a trained chimpanzee. Should not the media have been impressed rather than amused when they discovered that this so-called 'dumb' blonde could also love the poetry of W B Yeats and yearn to play a part in a film adaptation of Dostoevsky? It was perhaps one of

LEFT: Marilyn, as photographed in 1960.

ABOVE: DiMaggio and his son follow the funeral cortege.

the legacies of the puritanical 1950s that, as Arthur Miller remarked, the American psyche could not accommodate the co-existence of sexuality and seriousness, least of all in the same person. In the following decade of feminism and sexual liberation, Marilyn might well have been listened to more attentively.

Marilyn the star and Marilyn the actress are further contrasting, or conflicting, facets of her personality that are difficult to reconcile. Of course, she stood out in the 1950s from everyone around her. She was the siren who did for blondes what Elizabeth Taylor did for brunettes – only more so. Unlike Doris Day, she was the girl upstairs, not the girl next door. In contrast to the elfin sexlessness of Audrey Hepburn, she was the mistress of eroticism, but also a martyr to it. Unlike Grace Kelly's air of regal aloofness, Marilyn's manner had the common touch – but a touch that could still bedazzle royalty. As illustrated by Kim Novak (sexuality as subdued sultriness) and Jayne Mansfield (cleavage as caricature), Marilyn could be imitated, but she could not be equalled, and like Garbo, seemed almost to transcend critical analysis. Still the question seems to hover in the air: how good was she really?

'I don't think Marilyn had a great talent,' said Jack Lemmon, 'what she had was an ability to use completely the talents she did have.' Olivier grumbled that she was simply a model; George Cukor thought it was a trick of the light; and even a friend like Simone Signoret could not understand why Marilyn derived less satisfaction from her performances than from her poses (as in the series of photographs she had done with Richard Avedon, impersonating the stars of the 1930s). While Sartre and Strasberg were embracing her as a celluloid Bernhardt, Billy Wilder was discovering it took nearly 60 takes for her to say three words in the correct order. Yet, as he freely conceded, she could still produce a more magical performance without knowing her lines or even what day it was than most classically trained actors who arrive letter-perfect. It hardly seemed fair, did it?

How one wishes there was an acid test of her acting talent. There are roles in which one would love to have seen her. What about Monroe as Hitchcock's Marnie, tuning in to that character's childhood trauma, her obsessive and religious mother, and even to the director's fetish for blondes? Or as Tennessee Williams' Blanche DuBois, with Marilyn empathizing with that tragic character's desperate illusions, her horror at male brutishness, her reliance on the kindness of strangers? As for Lady Macbeth – seductress, sleepwalker and suicide – Marilyn, alas, only got to play her in real life.

If there is no concensus on Marilyn's acting abilities, there is a measure of agreement that her life, on the whole, was tragic. But what sort of tragedy was it?

Some have argued it as a specifically American tragedy. The scale and impact of her success could only have happened in America. However, like so many American success stories, it was short-lived. The flame burned more brightly than any, but burned out more quickly than most. Like the heroine of Henry James's classic novel *Daisy Miller*, Marilyn's fate was to suffer an archetypally American young death, with the promise only half-fulfilled and the character dazzlingly seen but not really known.

Or maybe Marilyn was a victim of Hollywood. She was destroyed by the studio system, so the argument goes, for she was shackled by a contract that undervalued her worth; she was pushed into inferior roles which projected an image of herself she came to dislike; and she was pitilessly discarded when she most needed support. Yet Hollywood insiders like Joseph L Mankiewicz and Billy Wilder have queried this interpretation. Mankiewicz has argued that the fabulous fame Hollywood helped manufacture for her cushioned the tragedy of her life rather than accentuated it. Wilder has always protested at the portrait of Marilyn as Tinseltown's sacrificial lamb. 'Let me tell you,' he said once, 'she was the meanest woman I have ever known in this town. I have never met anyone as utterly mean as Marilyn Monroe – nor as utterly fabulous on the screen.'

Feminists have come to regard the Monroe saga as a kind of biological tragedy, the kind that only happens to women. Marilyn paid the price of America's sexual immaturity. Her beauty and allure were the attributes that attracted attention but correspondingly precluded respect. She was treated as an object more than a subject. She represented the woman as spectacle, the body as trap. She became the prisoner of gender.

For Arthur Miller and others, her story seemed more like Greek tragedy – a foregone conclusion from the moment of her inception. She was the sport of her mad mother, and the people she encountered most closely in her life were members of a wailing chorus who could temporarily provide comfort but could not divert her from disaster. From the mid-1950s onwards, with Marilyn's grisly pile-up of divorces, miscarriages, scandals and breakdowns, even the dim-witted press seemed to wake up to the fact that a myth was malfunctioning. The writing about Marilyn became increasingly apocalyptic, as reporters listened to the agitated ticking of a sex-bomb about to implode.

Her life was a tragedy – but it could have been worse. Not many tragedies not only touch the hearts of millions but also make them smile. The comparison that springs to mind is Chaplin, who drew matchless comedy from out of his personal experience of hideous poverty. Marilyn somehow brought forth a breeze of innocence out of the Freudian nightmare of her childhood. Even when her image was part of the problem, she never lost the gift of sending it up. Even when cast as the plaything of a chauvinistic society, she found room to poke fun at both its norms and its neuroses. Even though she was a woman who could not bear too much reality, no-one seemed readier to expose herself on film, the camera always her most trusted confessor.

We now know that, in private, death was her constant companion, but on screen she never seemed less than life-affirming. It is the final paradox of her life and career. 'Here's to your life, Roslyn,' says Eli Wallach's character in *The Misfits*, 'I hope it goes on for ever.' It is a poignant line if applied to the real Marilyn, who had but two years left, but it is prophetic when applied to the Marilyn of the movies, now indisputably one of the screen's immortals.

LEFT: Official guests gathered at the ceremonies in front of the crypt as the body is deposited.

OVERLEAF: Marilyn waves goodbye from a taxi during her visit to London in 1956.

Index

Figures in italics refer to photographs. M. = Marilyn Monroe.

ACKNOWLEDGMENTS

The publisher would like to thank Design 23, Emma Callery the editor, Mandy Little the picture researcher, George Zeno for all his assistance and the following agencies and individuals for supplying the photographs:

AMPAS, pages: 24, 48 (bottom both), 49 (bottom both), 53, 57 (both), 81
Cecil Beaton Archive/Sotheby's London, page: 7
Bettman Archive, pages: 20, 21 (bottom), 68, 70, 76 (bottom), 77 (both), 92, 93, 95 (right), 112
Camera Press, pages: 2-3, 13, 28, 62, 63, 74, 78, 83, 102 (both), 103
Joel Finler Collection, pages: 1, 26, 33 (top), 35, 36, 38, 39, 50, 51 (top), 54, (bottom), 56 (top), 61, 75 (both)
Hulton Picture Company, pages: 11, 55
Robert Hunt Library, pages: 49 (top), 95 (left), 96, 97, 105, 108, 109
Keystone Collection, pages: 71, 72, 82, 89 (top), 98, 101
The Kobal Collection, pages: 8 (both), 9, 10, 18, 47, 94
Magnum Photos Ltd, page: 89 (bottom)
National Film Archive, London, pages: 32, 34, 37 (both), 41, 52, (both), 56 (both), 65 (bottom), 79, 80, 90, 91, 104
Photosource, page: 6
Topham Picture Library, pages: 12, 44, 54 (top), 58-9, 60 (top), 64, 65 (top), 99, 100
© Bob Willoughby, 1960, pages: 4, 84, 86 (both), 87 (both), 88
George Zeno Collection, pages: 5, 15, 16, 17, 19, 21 (top), 22, 27, 29, 30 (both), 31, 33 (bottom), 40, 42, 43, 45, 46, 51 (bottom), 58, 60 (bottom), 66 (both), 67, 69, 73, 76 (top), 106